When We Had It Made

Growing Up in the 50's & 60's in Small Town America

By Michael J. Colasurdo

Copyright © 2016 Michael J. Colasurdo

All rights reserved.

ISBN: 1535162511
ISBN-13: 978-1535162517

DEDICATION

I dedicate this book to my loving children and grandchildren, who have inspired me to share my childhood memories.

- Michael J. Colasurdo

MICHAEL J. COLASURDO

When We Had it Made is the fun-filled memories of a boy growing up during the wonder years of the 50's and 60's in small town America.

"*Bobby Sox and Blue Jeans, Block Dances, James Dean, Dick Clark, American Bandstand, Free Spirits, Elvis and Rock n Roll!*"

MICHAEL J. COLASURDO

CONTENTS

	ACKNOWLEGEMENTS	i
	INTRODUCTION	1
	FORWARD	5
1	THE POLICE – TO PROTECT AND SERVE	17
2	CANADA'S ANNUAL GIFT – THE ARCTIC COLD WINTERS	23
3	SLEDDING ON VAN BUREN STREET HILL	33
4	THE LEGEND OF PEPPER McNEIL	39
5	AN ACT OF COURAGE GIVES BIRTH TO A LEGEND	45
6	OUR FIRST PUPPY	53
7	MISUNDERSTOOD MAX	57
8	GREAT ADVENTURES AT THE BOATHOUSES	63
9	OUR SOAPBOX BUGGY	67
10	BASEBALL AT CASTLE SCHOOL	75
11	DAD'S RULE	79
12	THE OLD Y.M.C.A.	85
13	THE GREAT DISCOVERIES	91
14	THE GRAIN ELEVATOR	101
15	SUMMER VACATION AT HATCH LAKE	105
16	THE COAL TRESTLE AND THE GREAT FONTANA	107

17	THE GREAT WHIFFLE BALL GAMES	117
18	THE 9-INCH STRONG-BERG CARLSON TV	123
19	THE JAMES FENIMORE COOPER HOUSE	129
20	THE GREAT BRIDGE EXPLORATIONS	133
21	FRANI HENDERSON'S GREAT PINTO	135
22	THE COLLEGE STABLES AT FALLBROOK	139
23	AN UNFORGETTABLE LESSON	147
24	THE INCREDIBLE BLIZZARD OF '58	153
25	ISH – THE SCARIEST DOG IN THE FLATS	163
26	THE BIG CIRCUS CAME TO TOWN	167
27	MR. AND MRS. MURPHY	171
28	THE ALMOST-GREAT WARLORDS	175
29	MACARTHUR STADIUM WITH THE MICK & WILLIE	183
30	LITTLE LEAGUE, WHERE DREAMS CAME TRUE	187
31	AFTER LITTLE LEAGUE CAME BABE RUTH LEAGUE	193
32	WATER SKIING ON LAKE ONTARIO	197
33	KPS AND JR. HIGH SCHOOL	205
34	ICE SKATING AT THE KPS RINK	209
35	FRIDAYS MEANT CAHILL'S FISH DINNER	211
36	RUDY'S MILLION DOLLAR HOT DOG STAND	215
37	THE TEXAS HOT CHALLENGE	219
38	OSWEGO LEGEND – COACH DAVID E. POWERS	223

39	OSWEGO HIGH SCHOOL VARSITY FOOTBALL	233
40	ENTER "BA" AND SOME BROKEN BONES	239
41	THE GREAT ROCK AND ROLL BANDS	243
42	THE FAMILY REUNIONS	249
43	A MYSTERIOUS DISCOVERY	251
44	THE HIGH SCHOOL YEARS	255
45	THE CONVERTIBLE JOCKS	261
46	OUR FAVORITE WATERING HOLES	263
47	FAIR HAVEN AND SORORITY CAMP	271
48	TIME OUT	273
49	AN UNEXPECTED DETOUR TO DESTINY	277
50	OUR SIBLINGS	283
51	IT WAS THE GREATEST OF TIMES	285
52	A BRIEF HISTORY OF HISTORIC OSWEGO, NY	289

ACKNOWLEDGMENTS

I would first like to acknowledge my wonderful parents. Without them, I would not have the character they instilled within me or lived the happy and fulfilled life I have.

Thanks also to my brothers Tyrone and Frank and their wives, Sheryl and Debbie, for all that they have contributed to my life, especially in my time of illness.

I would like to thank all my friends I grew up with that have given me endless laughter, unending joy and lifelong friendships.

Thank you to my children and grandchildren for their love and support. Last but far from least, many thanks to my daughter, Angela, who has helped me to make this the fun read that it is.

And lastly, Joe Abbate, the expert technician, for his help in bringing the book to life.

Thank you to my family and friends for providing me with such great material from which to draw. You all hold a special place in my heart. I will never forget any of you, or our times *When We Had It Made*.

INTRODUCTION

Within these pages are some of the exciting tales of some of my childhood adventures during the greatest time in all of history to be young. I hope that some of my memories will ignite some of your own and will bring a smile to your face. Allow yourself to be transported back through the wonder years of the 1950's and 1960's when every day was an adventure in the small towns of America.

Back in the day, life was much simpler. People had respect for each other and we were free to come and go as we pleased with few restrictions as we had the greatest of times.

Our parents instilled within us confidence, respect and courage and we believed we could grow up to be anyone or do anything if we just worked hard and obeyed the rules. The working hard turned out to be much easier than obeying the rules as there was James Dean, Rock and Roll and a rebellious desire that stirred our young emotions.

These stories are a collection of some of my fondest memories growing up in small town USA. The small towns across America in the 50's and 60's, created the greatest time and place to be young. As my old friend, Billy McNaughton has said repeatedly, "We hit it just right. We were born at the greatest time in all of history."

There were the unmistakable feelings of genuine happiness that was a part of our everyday lives growing up in a small community. There were the fun filled adventures that would appear suddenly and without notice that provided laughter and entertainment because we were confident and unafraid.

I am sure that anyone who saw the movie *American Graffiti* or that was born during the Baby Boomer era would have to agree that life was very much the same for so many small towns throughout America during the truly good old days when we had it made.

The movie *American Graffiti* gained such great popularity because it hit home with so many young Baby Boomers that actually lived the stories that took place in that movie. It was a great portrayal of the young teenagers in America and their daily quest to seek out fun and laughter.

Just like me, they were fortunate to grow up in these small storybook towns like my own small hometown of Oswego, New York where my friends and I experienced the wonders of growing up during the most cherished times of our lives.

One of the commonalities of these small communities was that the people in each neighborhood knew just about everyone by their first name. This would prove to be a great advantage over those who lived in the much larger cities; these close relationships gave everyone a feeling of security and being in control of their own environment. This in turn created a strong level of comfort and confidence. It was also the basis for strong bonding that big city dwellers may have not have experienced to the degree that we did in the smaller communities.

Being brought up in a small community you learned very quickly that everything you said and did had a witness and that witness more than likely knew your name. This fact created an environment where people grew up to be honest and forthright in their actions and dealings because no one wanted to be perceived in a bad light or have humorous stories told about them for any mischievous acts of deceit they may have committed during a moment of weakness.

This mindset would pay off in huge dividends throughout our youth and later on in our lives as adults.

Oswego, New York was like most other small towns where the majority of the residents have an honest, down to earth mentality accompanied by a great sense of humor that created a great environment to build lifelong friendships that would last throughout our lives and would get passed down from generation to generation.

The early days were also a place where practical jokes were commonplace and very few if any were ever exempt from being the target for the benefit of humor. If you lacked enough self-confidence to be able to laugh at yourself or did not have a thick skin, you would soon develop one. The close bonding of the hearty people of these small communities was evident and unmistakably present.

It has always been my personal belief that one of the additional and major contributing factors to the close bonding among the people of my own small hometown came about because of the brutally cold winters that are endured by all residents each winter season.

This factor would additionally bring the people together because it was a fact that every person in the community must endure the very same hardships of the harsh winters. It was an unwritten rule that we were all in this together, we would stick together and we would survive together.

The town's people were wholesome and brought up to respect their neighbors. It was a place where honesty and trust was commonplace not the exception to the rule. The hearty people of the small towns would always find the humorous side in just about anything that was all but tragic. This made for a very stress free environment and created the wonderful small town attitude and the basis for a happy, confident and fulfilled childhood and life.

During my own personal life, my work and my business has allowed me to live in many large cities in the United States, Europe and Asia and I have discovered that these wonderful qualities were only found in the people brought up in these small communities. The people who have been fortunate enough to be brought up in the small towns of America do not have the great stress or burdens of the big city dwellers. I truly believe that these factors are why people of small communities live longer and generally have a better quality of life.

It is not my intention to offend the people who grew up in large cities, for the larger cities most certainly have far more opportunities to offer than the small towns of America. It is that there are positives and negatives to both.

It was the opportunities offered by the big cities that were the driving force that withdrew me from my beloved small town of Oswego, New York. This was why I have lived in so many large cities not only in America, but in Europe and Asia, as well.

It is just my observation and personal opinion that small town life is much simpler and slower and has far less stress than the hustle and bustle of the faster moving lifestyles of the larger cities.

FORWARD

WHEN WE HAD IT MADE

GROWING UP IN THE 50'S & 60'S IN SMALL TOWN AMERICA

My story begins on a cold and snowy late afternoon on March 7, 1946 with Michael Lewis Colasurdo driving northbound on old Route 57 just south of Fulton, New York on a return trip to Oswego, New York.

His young wife Frances who was now in the later weeks of her pregnancy accompanied Mr. Colasurdo and she was struggling with the unseasonably cold weather. The old vehicle was very rough riding in her delicate condition. She would not complain to her husband who was trying to focus on the road, but he continuously glanced over at his young wife to be sure she was not struggling, as he tried to make the impossible task of making the ride as smooth as possible.

The old car was moving along at a relatively fair speed considering the conditions; however, it was a very bumpy ride due to the snow in the road and the rough riding automobile, which was proving to be a very painful experience for his wife in her final month of pregnancy.

Just outside of Fulton, New York, the rough riding automobile would slow down due to the increasingly poor visibility from the now increasing winds and snowfall.

Mr. and Mrs. Colasurdo were returning from an anniversary celebration for Michael's parents who lived on Lodi Street in Syracuse, N.Y.

Michael had five sisters and their family had immigrated from Syracusa Sicily, Italy many years before in 1903. Frances Colasurdo was now in her ninth month of pregnancy. Just as they entered Fulton, N.Y., suddenly her water broke. Mr. Colasurdo tried to remain calm, something he had learned to do while in the Army under heavy and deadly gun and mortar fire in the Philippines just a year before during WW2. He was displaying confidence to his young wife that all would be alright as they were not far from the Fulton Hospital, although she was now understandably nervous and uncomfortable due to the very bad weather conditions.

Michael knew that this was a very dangerous situation; he was now facing the real life fear of not finding the Fulton Hospital. The weather conditions had badly deteriorated to blizzard-like conditions and he did not want to stop the already slow moving vehicle. There was the strong possibility the old car would be stuck in the deepening snow. The fear of not being able to make it to the hospital in time for the baby's birth was a harrowing thought as the temperatures continued to drop and darkness was covering the already deteriorating visibility of the road.

Then suddenly, like a great gift of a miracle bestowed upon them from the heavens above, the winds and snow just stopped like someone blowing out a candle. Visibility was restored. During the next ten minutes, which at the time seemed much longer, the old car had found its way to the Fulton Hospital entrance where a few hours later Mrs. Colasurdo would give birth to her first son, whom she would name after her courageous husband Michael.

The child was a healthy nine pounds six ounces and it had been a very difficult delivery for the young woman with a petite frame measuring less than five feet.

My parents would tell me this story throughout my entire childhood, reminding me in a loving and joking manner that I had brought trouble right from the very start.

Safely back in Oswego the next day, my mother with her newborn in her arms, comfortably settled into their warm upstairs apartment while my father was hard at work as the general manager at the Oswego County Cleaners just below. The business was located on East Bridge St. between East 7th and East 8th Street on the north side of Bridge Street, which was the main street going through the small town.

There was a small apartment over the Oswego County Cleaners building, located over the word Oswego where we lived for the first four years of my life. It was a one-bedroom apartment possessing beautiful French doors and it had a unique charm and character that was unmistakable.

My mother would give birth to her second son Tyrone just 16 months later on July 27, 1947. On December 27, 1949, she would give birth to her third son two years and five months after Tyrone's birthday. My father would name his last son after his best friend in the Army, whose name was Frank. The small apartment had long since become far too cramped and crowded for our young family.

On the east side of the second floor apartment there was a door leading from the apartment out to the top of the roof over the dry cleaning establishment. When I had just turned four years of age in March of 1950, on a cold snowy day, I ventured out through that door and out onto the roof and over to the front of the building just a short distance away.

The wall around the top edge of the roof of the building was only twelve inches high with a slick ceramic tile surface around the top of it and covered with the new fallen snow made it even more slippery. My father was twelve feet below shoveling the sidewalk. As I leaned over the short wall to yell down to him, I slid over the side and into the large pile of soft snow my father had just piled there. Remarkably, I was uninjured; however, I am sure that the horrifying sight put a major strain on my father's heart and I am equally sure that incident was a major contributing factor for our quick move to our new home just a few months later.

After my father quickly scrambled to pick me up from the pile of snow, he hurriedly brought me back upstairs to the apartment, wrapped me in a warm blanket, and returned me to my mother who was now in hysterics. My father would immediately nail that door shut until we moved to our new home just a few months later.

My father would tell me many times during my youth that when he picked me up out of the snow bank where I had fallen I keep saying, "Do it again! Do it again!" Now I do not remember any of this of course as I had just turned four years of age, but my dad swore it to be true. As my dad never lied, and I never had any reason to doubt him.

That spring, we moved into what would be our family homestead at 20 West 3rd Street in Oswego. My younger brother Tyrone (who Mom had named after her favorite movie actor Tyrone Power) and I were enjoying our new and much larger home and our new baby brother Frankie that would be the last child for Michael and Frances Colasurdo. This would be the beginning of many great adventures and wonderful years growing up in "The Flats" of Oswego, N.Y. in the 1950's for the Colasurdo boys. We now had a real home and we loved our new house and neighborhood.

The Flats was a great place to grow up in the 50's & 60's

Our neighborhood was known as "The Flats" because it was all flat land along the west side of the river from Bridge St. north to the lake and from the river west to West 4th Street. It was a place where adventure and discovery was everywhere.

On the NW corner of West Third and Lake Street was where our neighborhood began. There was a big white house that belonged to the new Coast Guard Station that was being built less than one hundred yards to the north of Lake Street and one hundred thirty yards from our house. This stood on the shore of the historic Oswego Harbor where Fort Oswego once stood before being demolished by the French in 1756.

The Coast Guard Commanding Officer and his family occupied the corner house and their little boy was my brothers and my first best friend. My brother Tyrone, whose name I could not pronounce, so I called him Nonie, and I played together every day in our fenced in backyard with the Commanding Officer's son, Archie.

After the completion of the new Coast Guard Station, the Commander and his family moved out of the house and the Madison family purchased it.

After about five or six years, the Madison's would sell the house to Betty Donovan who remodeled the house inside. Mrs. Donovan also owned a senior care nursing home and was very financially successful. She was one of the nicest women I would ever meet in my life and I loved her like a close member of our own family.

Mrs. Donovan's son from her first marriage, Bobby Nash, was tragically killed playing football a year earlier for

Oswego State University. The university discontinued the football program immediately after that.

I can remember thinking how unbearable the pain and sorrow must have been for that kind woman to endure. She suffered the tragic loss of her only son just a year before and was all alone, as her husband had died just two years previously in an automobile accident. I have no doubt in my mind that Mrs. Donovan never recovered from the loss of her only child. I once asked my mother why Mrs. Donovan, who was all alone, would purchase such a large house and then spend so much money to remodel it. The house had just been remodeled a few years previously and Mom said she had money and she was just trying to keep her mind busy to help keep from thinking about her son's death.

Some things in life are just too much to bear and the loss of a child has to be the worst pain of all life's horrible injustices.

I can remember sitting in our backyard and seeing Mrs. Donovan through her kitchen window sitting at her kitchen table sobbing as she had taken to alcohol to try to drown her never-ending heartsickness over the loss of her beloved son. I can remember the sick feeling I had for her as I watched her sobbing and praying I would never have to experience that kind of tragic pain in my own life.

It was painful for me to sit and watch that poor woman in such agony. I walked over to her back porch and opened her kitchen door as she sat crying uncontrollably. When I entered the room, she stood and we just wrapped our arms around each other. Without a word, we just squeezed each other. I held her as tightly as I could and we both cried for some time.

Mrs. Donovan would soon sell the house to Jimmy Barbera and his family whose dad owned the IGA grocery store at the Forks of the Road. Mom would tell me that Betty just could not bear watching all the children in the neighborhood because they were a constant reminder of the loss of her son and the horrible pain she just could not escape.

My mother would also tell me not long after that that Betty Donovan had died. When I asked my mother what was the cause she said Betty just could not stand any more of the pain of her broken heart and so, it just gave out. Then, Mom and I both hugged each other tightly as we thought of our friend and neighbor who was now with her son again. At last, she was without the agonizing pain that had tormented the kind woman for so long.

Mr. and Mrs. Barbara and their two toddler children would stay in the home for many years and they too were wonderful people and good neighbors.

The rest of the houses in the neighborhood were the homesteads of the families that would raise their children for many years to come. Most all of the parents in the neighborhood would spend the rest of their lives in their homes in the Flats of Oswego.

Our house was one house north of the corner Coast Guard house, as we always referred to it, and the neighborhood was plentiful with young Baby Boomer children.

On the northeast corner of West Third and Lake Street was the Baker's small home and to the best of my memory, they had eighteen children ranging in age from their late twenties to the youngest of three years. As a young boy living directly across the street from the Baker's small home, whenever I looked across the street all I could ever think about was the children's story, "The little old woman who lived in a shoe who had so many children she didn't know what to do" because there were kids everywhere all the time. Mrs. Baker would bake twenty loaves of bread every day of the week just to feed her family.

The neighborhood was swarming with children our age. There must have been seventy-five children within a two-block radius of West Third and Lake Street. It was undeniably the Baby Boomers era in full bloom.

The Finn's were in back of our house facing West 4th St. Next to them were the wonderful elderly couple Mr. and Mrs. Joyce who had two beautiful daughters Florence and Nancy who were about twenty years older than me. They were the most beautiful girls in all of Oswego and they looked like real life movie stars. The beautiful Florence married the wealthy Charles Saladin and Nancy married Joe Roedac a handsome and prominent attorney practicing law in Oswego.

Every day the neighborhood air filled with wonderful aromas from Mrs. Joyce's oven and her homemade bread and cakes.

I would from time to time go and sit on the Joyce's side porch. Mr. Joyce would see me sitting on his porch and he knew why I was there. He would come out and hand me a big slice of his wife's delicious fresh baked bread still hot from the oven dripping with real butter and a glass of milk. Every time, he would say to me, "Mikey, can you help me out here? I can't finish this piece of bread. Can you finish it for me so Mrs. Joyce doesn't get mad at me for not finishing her bread?" I would smile and say, "Sure, Mr. Joyce, I can help you out." I have no idea how many times I went through that conversation with the delightful old man, but you could see me perched on the Joyce's steps most days around ten a.m. whenever I was hungry.

They were wonderful people and I loved to help Mr. Joyce get rid of their extra bread and milk. My mother would also buy two loaves of Mrs. Joyce's bread every day and it was so good we ate every bite. However, Mom insisted on making all our birthday cakes and she could bake great, too.

In the 50's there were children's activities everywhere you looked on West Third Street and most of it took place right in front of the Colasurdo's home at 20 West 3rd St. There were many more families in the neighborhood and the children just kept on turning up. It was a grand place for young boys and girls to grow up, as there was never a shortage of playmates or games to be played.

As we grew in age, the Flat's was a wonderland of discovery. We were only two stone throws from the lake and a driver and a wedge from the river and there was adventure everywhere. The boathouses were a couple nine irons away from our front porch and that was a favorite place for fishing and swimming for all the kids in the neighborhood.

It was a wondrous place for children growing up.

1 THE POLICE – TO PROTECT AND SERVE

One of my favorite things we did in our youth was to build a Kainkee tree house in the big tree behind Pospisles end boathouse next to the lake.

It was a major undertaking and we were prepared to use every possible resource at our disposal.

We first looked through every nook and cranny in the neighborhood for the materials we would need.

After two days of searching for the huge amount of materials we would need and coming up with very little, it was becoming more than frustrating.

On the third day of our hunt for material, we stood in front of the huge tree thinking that this may be an impossible task. As we looked at the tree, I suddenly spotted about one hundred and fifty yards down the dirt road running parallel with the boat houses, a very large pile of materials piled alongside the boathouse road. When we got closer, our eyes and excitement grew as we suddenly realized here was everything we would need to build our tree house just one hundred yards away.

Someone had remodeled their boathouse and left this pile of materials along the side of the road. Here was everything we needed, even some 8 ft. by 4 ft. tin sheets that would be great for the siding and roof.

Charley Celestin came out of the newly remodeled boathouse and said, "Can I help you boys?" We all said, "Oh, yes sir!" We immediately asked the owner of the remodeled boathouse if he wanted that material. When he asked us why, we explained our need for the materials and asked if we could remove the entire pile for him. He said we could, as he was glad to get rid of it.

We dragged the entire pile of materials piece by piece over to the tree just one hundred and fifty yards away and we went to work.

I had asked my dad's permission to use his tools for our project and he agreed as long as I made a list of whatever I borrowed and gave that list to him so he could check to made sure we returned each item. Rest assured, he would be checking to make sure we did. He also gave me a big carpenter's nail box that had all sized nails and it must have weighed thirty-five or forty pounds. We loaded the tools and the heavy nail box onto our red flyer wagon and we were off to enter the business of Kainkee tree house construction.

We nailed the 2 by 6 boards for the base of the tree house floor on the big tree branches. We nailed two by 4's to the sides of the tree house and to the roof. We nailed down the sides and the roof with the metal sheets using Dad's big twenty-foot extension ladder. That was a load to handle, but we worked together as a group and with the use of a rope, we managed to handle the long and very heavy old wooden extension ladder.

After several days of construction, it was completed and we could not have been more proud of what we had accomplished. It was a grand tree house and we did it all by ourselves.

Dad was very pleased that the entire list of his tools had been returned, covered with 10/20 motor oil to prevent rust, and put away.

Early the next morning, our gang was walking down the road on our way to spend the morning at our new clubhouse in the tree. Just as we approached the tree house, we could see through the open window of the tree house that someone was inside. Who could this intruder be? When the man spotted us, he, in a very gruff voice, told us to go away and not come back because this was now his house and any intruders would suffer.

We were in shock! This hobo was taking up residence in our new clubhouse. As we walked back up Lake Street, a police patrol car came by and we flagged him down and explained our unjust dilemma and the uninvited "king of the road" who now occupied our new Kainkee tree house.

The officer said, "I will take care of this, boys." He drove over to the tree house with our gang running in tow.

Back at the Kainkee clubhouse, the police officer summoned the hobo to come down and told him to get in the patrol car and he would then take him to jail or to the outskirts of town, it was his choice. He then told us to reoccupy our clubhouse, which we excitedly and quickly did.

We would discover the next day when our new hero officer friendly came by to see how we were doing that he had taken the hobo to the city limits after stopping at George's Delicatessen on West Bridge St. to buy the man a sack lunch for his journey.

In those days, the patrol cars had written on their fenders "To Protect and Serve" and they meant it.

When you look back at the simplicity of our childhood, it was a wondrous time. We had the freedom to do whatever we wanted to do and the adventurous nature that was usually required to do it.

If, for some reason, a police officer would have to show up due to our behavior or actions, they never wanted to make a big deal out of it or try to intimidate us. The police officers would listen to our story. The officer would then pile us into the cruiser and take us home to confront our parents. This would end with a warning. This only happened a few times and usually because we were somewhere, we should not have been -- like the time I was on top of Castle School retrieving baseballs that at some point in the past had been the results of a well- struck homerun.

I am certain that is why the people of Oswego and other small communities have much greater respect for their neighbors and the police and live simpler, happier, longer and far more fulfilled lives than those who have to experience the stress and dramas of larger city dwellings where many people live in fear.

2 CANADA'S ANNUAL GIFT – THE ARCTIC COLD WINTERS

The one thing you could be sure of living in Oswego, New York was when the leaves turned a thousand different colors in the fall, a brutally cold winter was soon to follow. However; the fall was a beautiful time of the year as the strong winds would increase, separating the leaves from the trees and sending them swirling into the air until they would eventually succumb to gravity and lay upon the ground until the next gust of strong wind would again send them swirling into the air.

These would be the early warning signs that you were about to spend a long and very cold winter as the arctic winds could reach speeds of fifty to sixty miles per hour as they swept down out of Canada, picking up speed as they crossed the vast waters of Lake Ontario.

Those first cutting winds were soon followed by four to five months of an extremely cold winter that would deposit over one hundred inches of snow annually. These would leave the small town buried in snow and the shores of southeastern Lake Ontario a frozen wonderland. The hearty people of Oswego must contend with and endure these fierce winter conditions each winter.

These powerful winds would at times send twenty to thirty foot waves smashing into the ice-covered breakwater wall that guarded Oswego's Harbor. It was a breathtaking explosion of brilliant silver spray as high as forty to fifty feet into the air creating an exciting and wondrous spectacle that would leave me in awe, as I would watch nature's devastating winter fury. This awesome sight has never escaped my mind.

At the far end of this ice-covered break wall there is a majestic old Light House. Built in 1934, it houses the beacon that marks the entrance to the Oswego Harbor and the lifeline for the ships in the night that navigate a sometimes violent and very dangerous Lake Ontario. Each winter this weather-beaten lighthouse supported tons of ice several feet thick long before the spring thaw. In the 1950's and 60's and long before, it was and still is an annual event for the Oswego River, Harbor and the southern shore of Lake Ontario to be covered with ice. In most places along the shore to the east and west of Oswego's breakwater wall, there would be mountains of thick ice many feet thick.

The frozen harbor would support those brave enough to fish upon the ice in their portable little houses built on two by six board runners, allowing the little shelters to be pushed across the ice to their favorite fishing location. The little shacks had no floor; the anglers would cut holes in the ice with a pickax or usually a chainsaw then pull the little shelters over the hole so that they might go after their catch of the day while being sheltered from the harsh cutting winds that blew in from the north. Many of the shacks had metal buckets filled with coal from the many trains on the tracks until the spring when the coal boats would return. The little buckets would provide plenty of heat to fight off the bitter cold as well as supplying the fire to cook the fish caught right then.

My parents would look us straight in the eye and swear a solemn oath to cripple us for life if they ever even heard that we had ventured out onto that ice.

Even though it was a very rare occasion because the ice was usually very thick, there had been people over the years that had fallen through thin spots in the ice and drowned. That was more than enough for our parents to enforce the no ice rule.

Although, and very surprisingly to me, my mother would allow me to go ice fishing with my mentor and older cousin Pepper McNeil.

Mom had trusted her older sister Helen's only son, for he was a smart and responsible young man and he cared for me like the little brother that he never had.

As a young boy living not much more than one hundred yards from the Coast Guard Station docks and in clear sight of the breakwater wall, I would sit on our front sun porch that had a magnificent view of the harbor. I would watch the amazing show of the silver spray bursting high into the air above the breakwater wall that protected the inner harbor from those devastating waves that would otherwise have destroyed the shore of the inner harbor as it had done for thousands of years before.

Our sun porch was now enclosed with winter storm windows that my father would change every fall and replace with screened windows in the spring to allow the cool breeze off the lake to flow through the small rooms in the front of our home on a hot summer's evening.

During the warm summer nights, this was the very same location that my mother and father would sit in the evenings and sip their iced tea, lemonade or orange/lemonade while watching their sons and the neighborhood kids play Whiffle Ball. We played in the road in front of our house every evening, and this was without question my folk's favorite evening place to relax and Whiffle Ball was our favorite evening activity during these warm summer evenings.

During the winter months, I would wrap myself up in my mother's hand-stitched, multi-colored quilt comforter she had made many years before as a group project with her sisters as a family quilt. The old quilt was now old, tattered and torn and was very soft to the touch and my first choice since I had been a small child. I would additionally wrap an old Army blanket around me that would not allow my body heat from escaping. The two blankets provided ample comfort and warmth as I sat in the little frozen room watching what I thought was one of nature's greatest shows and it was free for the taking… if you could stand the very cold temperatures of our sun porch.

As I sat in the little unheated room, I would be mesmerized watching, as the huge waves would violently crash into the breakwater wall repeatedly. The explosions that sent the silver spray soaring high into the air and the strong winds from the northwest would carry the glistening spray far into the by now ice covered harbor.

Most of the spray sent high into the air would freeze while in flight and land like bouncing pellets on the frozen surface of the harbor ice. Some of the unfrozen water on top of the ice would soon freeze, adding to the already thickening ice.

The howling of the winds that sounded like a train roaring battered the north side of our house and would rattle the storm windows at times violently. To me, this was extremely exciting, and I would sit there watching this until I could no longer stand the cold of the small room or my mother would discover I was once again out in the very cold glass enclosure. Upon her discovery, she would make me come back into to the warmth of the heated living room for fear I would, "Catch my death of cold" as she had said perhaps a thousand times during my youth.

As I sat in that little room of frozen wonderment, I would wonder how many other people were fortunate enough to be watching this incredible display of nature's awesome power and beauty.

I can recall when I looked through the frozen windows that were now in the shape of a quarter-moon of frozen crystal that you could only see out the center portion of the windows from inside our sun porch. I wondered if others who did not have the fortunate view as I could see the amazing winter ritual that had been going on every winter since the mile high glacier that came slowly sliding down from Canada that carved our Lake Ontario some 12,000 years earlier.

It also appeared to me that at times, we were in a frozen capsule in time that dragged on for what seemed to be forever. I would on occasion prod my dad to heat that little room of frozen wonderment and he would say, "Son that is a sun porch, not a snow porch" and that would be the end of the conversation. Part of Dad's no-nonsense charm was the way he would always break things down to their simplest form. He was a no-nonsense kind of man and I liked that because he made things simple; simple makes the rules easy to understand and eliminates confusion, which prevents misunderstanding, and that was always a good thing.

Although as children, we never considered winter to be a hardship, in our young minds this winter wonderland presented many wonderful and exciting opportunities for fun and adventure. Our thoughts were any discomfort from the cold was the price we were willing to pay for the great fun we enjoyed in the snow and on the forbidden ice with my beloved big cousin Pepper. It just provided a time limit on how long we could play in the cold temperatures before the tingling of the fingers and toes set in and we would head for the warmth of Mom's kitchen oven and her always steaming hot cocoa and cookies that would be on the kitchen table awaiting her sons return to her side.

My mother would tell us every day without fail in her sternest motherly voice, "When your feet or hands start to tingle, you must come home immediately and I will have hot cocoa with baby marshmallows and fresh baked cookies still hot from my oven all ready for you!"

Mom knew that the thought of her delicious cookies and hot cocoa would bring us home long before giving in to the tingling of our cold toes or fingers. We knew from experience that following that tingling feeling was the burning sensation that would eventually lead to a very painful feeling of being frost bitten if not returned home to a hot bath. We were particularly careful not to stay out too long after that unwanted tingling feeling began.

I can only imagine that my memories were similar to those of my hearty friends. We all grew up and braved the violent winters of northern New York together. I also believe that is why the people of this very special little community had developed such a great bond and sense of humor. The people of my hometown could always find the comedy in just about any situation, forsaking the tragedies of life, even in the coldest of the great northern winters.

It was always fun for me growing up with my childhood friends, for we laughed all the time because we always sought out the humor in all we did. After all, we were just children and we were all about fun.

It was a grand childhood I shared with some wonderful friends who all developed great character and grew up to make their parents proud and raised wonderful families of their own to whom they passed along the very same small town values that their parents instilled in them. It was very simple. We never had to work at respecting and admiring our neighbors. We just did.

3 SLEDDING ON VAN BUREN STREET HILL

The first few feet of snow had fallen, usually sometime near the middle or end of December. Around the corner from our home, the city would block off the very steep Van Buren Street hill with barricades. Two official crossing guards, who were usually retired men, would guard the street. They kept a close, watchful eye on all of us for any intruding automobiles that might suddenly venture into our restricted area where so many children played in the road.

The city would hire the older men and stationed one at each intersection to ensure our safety. They were never without their large green metal coffee thermos bottles with the silver screw on top that doubled as a coffee cup. They would place a barricade on each side of Van Buren Street at the intersections of West 4th, West 5th Street and across Van

Buren at West 3rd St. and West Sixth Streets.

Under each barricade they placed a round metal ball that had a flame fueled by kerosene and produced a very bad odor.

To go west or up Van Buren Street hill in the dead of winter was an impossible task, even with snow tire chains which every car and truck had in the early 50's. Thus, the only real risk with cars was traffic going north and south on West Fourth and West Fifth streets and those were usually only the people living on those streets and our safety guards kept a keen eye out for those vehicles and our safety.

There were usually two safety guards on the hill. My Mom would always put out two large pieces of her fresh-from-the-oven baked banana bread or some other baked delight she had made that day. She would place a generous spread of real butter on the pastry, wrap it in waxed paper, place them in two separate brown paper sacks and direct me to give one to each of the old boys. She was always doing such kind acts for others, whether she knew them or not. That was just the way mom was; she truly cared about other people and was an exceptionally kind and generous woman who loved to see people enjoy the treasures from her oven. Her treats would bring joy to your mouth and always produced a smile.

Van Buren Street hill was a great place for sledding, tobogganing and the new aluminum saucers that you could not steer or control. On occasion, they would go over a jump that would send the children aboard flying and tumbling head over heels into a frosty snow covered end.

Van Buren Street was a very steep hill especially from West 5th down to West 4th St., and we would be thrilled when taking flight over the big snow jumps we had built up and reinforced in front of the Peterson home each evening many times. We would pack the snow tightly and the jumps would eventually be reduced to small bumps as the runners of the sleds would dig into the snow and eventually destroy the jumps until we would rebuild them once again.

These snow jumps were located at the steepest section of the hill in between West 4th and West 5th Streets. When the children's sleds landed, they would usually flip over and they would go tumbling into the snow, which brought on great peals of laughter to all who were witness. Our tumbles would also produce some minor black and blue marks, but of course, no one would complain because we were having far too much fun to consider any such small body discomforts. That was of course until we got home when Mom would undress us to give us her complete once over inspection to see if we were the same as when she had last bundled us up in clothing in which you could hardly walk. The problem with the heavy and tight winter clothing was trying to get back upright after a tumble into the snow. This was no easy task and always required assistance for the smaller children; however, watching the little tots struggle to get upright held its own form of humor.

Those bulky clothes kept us very warm and were a great cushion when we went tumbling head over heels into the snow on a failed landing attempt after our sleds had completed their flight from the jump.

After the last slide down the hill, our fingers and toes would always be tingling from the cold. I would put my two little brothers, who were by now both exhausted; onto my long Flyer sled and drag them home with their smaller Flyers behind us in tow. Their little boy voices would always yell,

"Faster, horsey, faster!"

When we arrived back home, Mom would undress the two little boys and wrap them in warm blankets. Mom would have homemade cookies and steaming hot cocoa with little baby marshmallows floating on top all ready for us on the kitchen table. The open door of her oven sent out waves of heat that keep her sons as warm as possible. We would all hover around the open oven door to get as close to the heat that warmed us. We smiled with joy as we ate the mouthwatering cookies from Mom's oven and sipped the hot cocoa. Then Mom would put us in a hot bath and after a thorough toweling to dry us off, she would quickly zip us into our PJ's and the wonderful woman would kiss us and send us off to bed to dream of the great fun we had had sledding down Van Buren Street hill.

We would stop at Dad's favorite chair as he watched the small television set to kiss him good night and then up the stairs we would go, to fall fast asleep to dream of the great fun sledding on Van Buren Street hill and the exciting flights after leaving each snow jump.

In my dreams, after leaving the snow jump, I would continue to fly high over the rooftops with my two small brothers sitting in front of me between my legs as I navigated my airborne American Flyer. We would fly high over the rooftops of the neighborhood and across the frozen river and bridges and back again. My little brothers would be so proud of their older brother for he was the only person they knew other than Superman that was capable of flight.

The wonderful childhood imagination that would bring so much fascination to my youth would mysteriously just vanish over the years. However, being able to fly was a regular dream that I had from childhood until late into my teens. I don't know what that meant, but I loved those dreams and I can only hope that one night they will return, while I am fast asleep so that I might once again be transported back to those magical childhood years growing up in the 50's and 60's in small town America.

MICHAEL J. COLASURDO

4 THE LEGEND OF PEPPER McNEIL

My cousin and mentor Bobby "Pepper" McNeil was a real life legend in the small town of Oswego, New York in the 1950's. Pepper was "all boy" and as he grew older, he would become a man's man. My mother's older sister, my beloved Aunt Helen, whom we all called Aunt Honey, raised him. She was the second eldest of the Knopp sisters and dearly loved by all in the family.

Aunt Helen also had four beautiful daughters Barbra, Ann, Nancy and Joann (whom we called Jodi) and they were all very beautiful young girls who grew up to be elegant women who all raised beautiful families of their own. I used to like to go to Aunt Helen's house to visit. Her daughters Nancy, Jodi, and our cousins Diane and Darlene Frye, who lived just a city street away from Aunt Helen's house, and I were all around the same age and we would play our children's games in my Aunt Helen's house and backyard.

The girls were great fun and I loved them all like my own sisters.

My cousin Pepper, who was seven or eight years older than me, was a very knowledgeable woodsman and hunter and he could do anything he put his mind to. Pepper would take game from the woods on a daily basis and we would always have some great wild game or fish dinners at my Aunt Helen's house.

There was a small shed at the back of my Aunt Helen's house. One day, when I was about eight years of age, my beloved cousin Pepper called the girls and me to see what he had in the shed. When he opened the door to that small room that led to the cellar, right there on the cement floor lay two dead possums he had shot the night before on one of his evening hunts in the woods. The girls screamed and ran away while I looked on in shock. Pepper just laughed and said, "That's dinner tonight, Mikey!" I said, "Maybe for you, Pep, but not for me! I am gonna eat at my mom's house tonight."

My Aunt Helen once instructed Pepper to kill two chickens from the chicken coop in the backyard for the dinner meal. Pepper said to me, "C'mon, Mikey!" and took me by the hand to the backyard. He advised me to sit me down next to the shed and he instructed me not to move and to pay attention for this was something every young boy needed to know how to do.

He then tied one chicken by its legs to a clothesline while the bird screeched as though it knew what was about to happen. The second chicken he held by its head and laid it over the stump of a tree he used for a chopping block. He then swiftly chopped the head off the chicken on the stump and then turned with the speed and precisioned accuracy of a seasoned ninja warrior to cut off the head of the chicken on the clothesline. The headless chicken on the ground ran completely around the yard making its final tour of the backyard spouting blood from its neck, while the chicken on the clothesline flapped its wings as it flew over and around that clothesline several times spraying blood eveywhere before its final demise.

It was like mass hysteria as I looked on in bug-eyed amazement and terror. Pepper said, "You see, Mikey, chickens do run around crazy with their heads cut off." I would never forget that. Throughout my life whenever anyone would use that old expresson, "running around like a chicken with its head cut off" the picture of my ninja-like cousin in his back yard decapitating screeching fowl would come immediately and vividly to the forefront of my mind.

That night at Aunt Helen's, the table was set with a delicious roasted chicken dinner with all the fixins. However, I only ate the mashed potatoes and gravy, for the sight of those two headless chickens making their final flight of the back yard was still crystal clear in my mind. That was more than enough to turn me off on a poultry dinner. Pepper and the girls would offer me chicken parts throughout the meal as they all laughed at the young boy who prior to this meal, had loved to eat chicken.

Pepper McNeil was an incredible young man; he was fearless, intelligent and a grand storyteller with a marvelous sense of humor. He would entertain the girls and I with his wonderful stories that would always make us laugh right from our bellies. Pepper just had an amazing way about him and had an infectious smile and laughter that drew you to him. He was a very likeable all American young boy with a very special charm that commanded your attention and affection.

Pepper also had an amazing dog named George that I called "George the Wonder Dog" because he was, and I loved being in both his and his master's presence whenever possible.

George was part German Shepard and part Sheepdog, but he looked more like a shorter version of a German Shepard. He was as smart a dog as there ever was.

There was a fence between my parent's house and our neighbors on West 3rd Street. My dad had built the fence a few years before and it was five feet high. George the Wonder Dog was only about eighteen inches high. That little dog could easily jump over that fence with just a short running start. George was an exceptionally intelligent canine, adding to the reasons I called him a wonder dog.

Pepper was a great master of the woods as we called the sparsely populated areas surrounding our small town. He hunted and he provided food for his mother's table on a daily basis. I would tell him in later years he should have been born one hundred years earlier, because he would have been a great pioneer of the great American wilderness.

Pepper loved to hunt but he did not hunt just for the

enjoyment of hunting. He hunted for food: rabbits, partridge, pheasant, squirrel, dear, possum and even raccoon. If it lived in the woods, it was a potential meal for cousin Pepper.

In the winter, Pepper would trap beaver and fox for their furs for extra money to help his mother with the household expenses. Everyone in the family loved the smiling freckled-faced good-natured young man with light brown dirty blond curly hair. He was my hero from day one and has been a part of me ever since. Cancer would take him from us when he was still just a young man. That would leave a huge void in all of us who loved him so dearly… and we all did.

5 AN ACT OF COURAGE GIVES BIRTH TO A LEGEND

In the above photo of 1950's Oswego, you can see the railroad bridge in the forefront that spans the Oswego River. On the left side of the photo next to the railroad bridge is the seven-story building of the Cyclotherm.

In 1950, just because no one had ever done it, and Pepper knew without question that he could, Robert "Pepper" McNeil would run across the top of the roof of the Cyclotherm building and leap to a ninety-foot drop. There was a cement wall of about twenty-five feet between the building and the canal water that he had to clear before smashing violently into the canal water. He hit the water under tremendous force that would leave his body black and blue from head to toe from the violent impact.

Pepper McNeil didn't realize it at the time, nor was it the reason that he did this, but that leap of courage would make him a legend in Oswego all throughout the 1950's and 60's until that building was eventually knocked down and the monument to his act of courage was no more.

Many teenage boys have leaped from the lower steel of the railroad bridge into the canal; a few have claimed they leaped from the top of the railroad bridge. However, Pepper McNeil was the only person ever to dare such a heroic and dangerous leap throughout all of the history of Oswego, New York and he did it because he knew it could be done – and he knew he could do it.

I was not present the day Pepper made this heroic and historic leap as I was only four years old at the time. However, my Aunt Helen who was the most honest woman I have ever known told me this story. Surely, this is the reason why all her children grew up to be of strong character and highly respectable adults.

Pepper did in fact make that incredible daring leap and when he got home with a trail of hero worshipers in tow, he was black and blue from his head to his toes.

Several others there that day were witness to his great deed and years later would confirm to me that they witnessed his incredible leap.

Dick Henderson, who would work with Pepper for several years for the city cutting down and trimming the great trees of the community, was also a lifelong friend of Pepper. He, too, was a witness and he told me that he witnessed the heroic event and that it was the greatest thing he had ever seen in all his life.

Ed "Tarzan" Brady, who Pepper once told me was the toughest man he ever knew (and in those days that was tough) would also tell me years later that he was also present at the time of Pepper's incredible leap. He also verified that Pepper made that great jump from the roof of the Cyclotherm building and he said he was there and watched the exceptional exhibition of courage and it was the bravest thing he had ever seen in his entire life.

Pepper once told me that Brady would not lie for love or for money. However, people also knew Ed Brady's favorite topics of conversation were about his own accomplishments. He was rarely known to credit or praise another.

I never understood Pep and Brady's friendship because Pepper was humble and would never brag about anything he had ever done. Ed Brady, on the other hand, was pretty much the opposite, although it was believed that Brady would never embellish a story either. It was a code of conduct the young men of that era shared. It was a shared respect they had for each other based on courage, honesty and integrity.

Pepper was my beloved mentor; he had a wonderful smile that was infectious and an exceptional sense of humor with a great laugh that made me laugh whenever I would hear it. He was honest, loyal, beloved and respected by all who ever knew him.

Pepper McNeil would never back down from a challenge. He was simply fun to be around and I worshipped the young man that had so much courage. Pepper was eight years older than me, and my mom's self-appointed big brother for me.

 My Mother, who also adored her older sister's son, would allow me to go anywhere with him because she had complete trust and confidence in the young man that was still in a young boy's body.

Pepper taught me to swim, fish and hunt while I was still very young. He taught me to have courage, to be honest, and to be respectful. He also taught me to never, under any circumstances, fear or back down from any challenge or threat. My cousin Ronnie Verdoliva and my father also instilled in me these very same values.

They all taught me self-confidence and to have respect for others. All of admirable qualities they instilled in me were a part of their own character and would serve me well in my journey through adolescence and life.

When I was six years old, my cousin Pepper took me fishing in a rowboat one hundred yards offshore at the boathouses. George the Wonder Dog sat at my feet in the boat. After we had fished for some time and the hot late morning sun was bearing down on us, Pepper looked down at me and said, "Mikey, have you learned to swim yet?" I answered, "No, Pep, I am only six years old."

With that, he reached over, snatched me up and pitched me into water that was far over my head. I came up splashing and gasping. Pepper stood in the small boat and yelled to me, "Swim, Mikey! Move your arms like this!" He made a swimming motion. "Kick your legs!" he continued. Suddenly, George the Wonder Dog barked and then leaped into the water after me. In a flash, Pepper pulled the wonder dog and me back into the boat. Then Pepper said, "That was your first swimming lesson!"

Years later, at the age of fifteen, I would swim from the coal trestle out around the lighthouse and then east along the long breakwater wall to Sheldon's beach. I would guess that the distance would be about three miles. However, it certainly seemed to be much longer than that at the time. I just did it to see if I could.

Pepper also took me ice fishing. We pulled a little ice-fishing house built just for that purpose that he had borrowed from a friend at the boathouses and we had a great time fishing on the ice. Without Pepper's guidance, this was a forbidden place for me to go.

Pepper chopped out a hole in the ice with a pickax, and we

pulled the little house over the hole and started a fire in a metal pot. That provided heat. We placed a metal screen on top of that little bucket that now doubled as a barbeque pit that also kept us toasty warm inside that little house. It got so warm we could take off our overcoats and it kept the hole in the ice from freezing over, too. When we would catch a fish (of which we caught many) Pep would say, "There ain't a lot of bugs fallin' through the ice in the winter, so the fish are pretty hungry. They will even bite on a bare hook," And then he proved it to me by catching a big Jack Perch with just a bare hook.

Pep would then fillet the fish on the spot in just about a minute with his razor sharp hunting knife and his skilled hands that had completed that task so many times before. Pep always had his razor sharp bone handled hunting knife strapped to his side while fishing or hunting, because the game had to be cleaned immediately. The smell would be overwhelming if you waited until later, as he had preached to me so many times before.

Then in the wink of an eye, he would flip the now boneless fish into a skillet. Pep would cook and we would eat right there and then. Pepper would say, "It does not get any fresher than this, Mikey!" We would laugh and George the Wonder Dog would eat his fill, too, for we would catch many fish.

We would also bring home a stringer full of perch and Pepper even caught a large Great Northern Pike. It was great day fishing on the ice far out in the harbor and I had the greatest time with my mentor and hero.

When I was twelve, Pepper took me to get a hunting license. The next day, he came to my house bright and early in the morning. With him, he carried two shotguns, and one was for me. Pepper was with old Boots Peterson and his son, Jimmy. Jimmy was a few years younger than Pepper; however, Jimmy had a car and would drive us to the woods almost every weekend in the fall and winter where we never failed to shoot game.

On this day, we were off for my first lesson with firearms. This would be my first of many hunting trips with these three men. We would have the greatest times in the woods. We hunted together and we always ate wonderful game meals because they were all crack shots and rarely missed an opportunity- even with a difficult shot like a partridge which fly very fast and never in a straight line or elevation.

Pepper was a store of knowledge when it came to the woods and its creatures, and he delighted in teaching me his vast knowledge. I will admit I never did like the cleaning of the game we shot, but Pep insisted that this was part of being a hunter, so I would do it and not complain.

In later years, Pepper and I were sitting in the shade under a tree in my favorite place atop the Lake Street bank where I had spent a lot of time dreaming my young boy fantasies. As we lay there under the shade tree enjoying the cool breeze that came off the lake, I looked up at Pepper and I asked, "Why did you really make that dangerous jump off the old Cyclotherm?" He looked at me and said, "I guess it was because everyone else thought that it was impossible to do. I knew I could do it, so I had to do it to prove it."

Then I said, "Why would you do something so dangerous just to prove to others that it could be done? Pepper never blinked or hesitated, but said, "Mikey, I did not care what they thought. I did it because I had to prove it to myself." I never doubted his statement because that was exactly the kind of young man this remarkable person was.

Pepper died of cancer as a young man far before his time. With him, died a large piece of so many of us that loved him, especially his sisters who adored him as much as I did.

I was proud to be his chosen personal understudy; to be mentored by him; to be as close to him as I was; and most importantly, just proud to be his friend. He was one of Oswego's greatest sons of all time. Pepper was a constant display of pride and character and I dearly loved him like my very own big brother.

I was greatly blessed to have had Pepper McNeil in my life!

RIP my beloved brother.

6 OUR FIRST PUPPY

I can remember the overwhelming feelings of happiness and joy that came over my younger brothers and me when my dad first brought home the wonderful gift of our first puppy. We stroked our soft and cuddly little four-legged friend. My new companion would be dependent upon me for all her needs and I would always be there for her without fail.

My parents were well aware of the importance of this bonding relationship that would take place between this little puppy and my brothers and me, but it was unknown to us at the time what a huge part it would play in the development of our personalities, character and especially our emotions.

That very first day and forever after, we would play for hours on end with my little friend that would bring me such great joy and happiness. I do not think I ever stopped smiling. I do not think there is anything that compares to a young child playing with their very first puppy. It was a wonderful feeling of complete and true happiness.

I would have many other puppies over the decades of my life and enjoyed playing with every one, for each was unique. However, nothing was ever quite as magical as playing with my first puppy. I believe that your first puppy is a vital part of your journey through adolescence.

We would go everywhere together; if you saw me, you saw my dog. If I lay down under a tree, she was at my side. If I jumped into the lake, she was right behind me. Wherever I went, she was right at my heels.

The gang would yell at her because when we played ball everyday my dog would chase after and get to the ball before the kids in the field. Then, she would pick it up between her teeth and bring it to me. We were inseparable. It was a wonderful relationship and my parents loved that beautiful Collie I named Sandy. I believed that that dog would protect me to her death.

One day, while going to the Acme Market for my mom, I crossed the road at West 2nd and West Seneca Street. My dog was investigating something with her nose, as dogs do, and she fell behind. When she came running to catch up with me, she ran into the road at West Seneca St. and was struck by a car and killed.

The incredible rush of emotions was something I could have never prepared myself for and would not soon forget. I was heartbroken and extremely upset for a very long, long time. In fact, the truth is, it still very much hurts me at this moment when I think about the day I lost my very first best friend.

My mom, who was also heartbroken over our loss, would ask me, "Mikey, do you want another puppy?" I said, "No, Mom. The loss of my friend just hurts too badly and I never want to feel that pain again."

My mother hugged me and said she understood and assured me I would be all right in time. Nothing is as soothing to a child as having their mother's arms drawn around them into their mother's bosom accompanied by those words,

"It will be all right."

7 MISUNDERSTOOD MAX

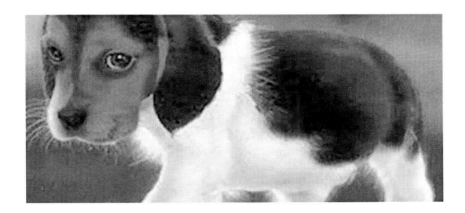

Years would go by before I would get my second puppy, and that was only because cousin Pepper said I needed a good Beagle to go with us when we hunted. My neighbor, Mr. Watts, who lived two houses up the street, had a Beagle that had just recently had puppies and said I could have one. The new Beagle puppy was as cute as could be. However, he would soon create problems at just about every turn and would lose a great alliance with Mom who would eventually turn against the short little Beagle with a knack for getting into trouble.

By the time Max was a year old, Mom and the neighbors all immensely disliked the little dog. It seemed everyday Max was developing more bad habits. The worst, and the one that would eventually do Max in, was his love of chasing Mom when she went out in our back yard to hang up her laundry on the clothesline. Max would go after her apron or her housedress; get the garments firmly in his mouth; and growl and tug at them until they would rip. That was more than Mom could tolerate from the little dog.

Max thought he was being playful, but Mom saw no humor with his behavior. Max would lose an ally in Mom that would prove to be his worst doggie nightmare.

The little dog also loved chasing cars and people; it was the little dog's passion all day, every day. The neighbors were not big fans of little Max, either. Max would chase everyone with only one exception, my cousin Jackie De Stevens, who lived across the street. Jackie had won Max over with some doggie treats he had for his own Beagle named Babe who was an excellent rabbit-hunting dog.

My brothers, Jackie and I would sit on our front steps and watch Max's antics. Our favorite happened to big Billy Musacchio. Billy was my age, my friend and my next-door neighbor. He was by far the biggest kid in all the Flats. Billy was over six feet tall and had a heavy frame that made him Max's favorite target. Billy had inherited that body frame from his father, who had a very similar build. Max would be hot after Billy at every given opportunity and Billy would run from the little dog that was not but twelve inches high and weighed maybe six pounds soaking wet.

We would laugh uncontrollably on the steps of our front porch as we watched little Max terrorize the boy who towered over him and outweighed him by two hundred and fifty pounds. Billy would run and leap over the short three-foot black metal fence that separated the two yards. The fence would shield Billy from the short misunderstood Max. That picture has popped up in my mind throughout the years and has always made me burst out in laughter at the memory.

One day while Max was chasing a car, he suffered a broken leg. My mother and all the neighbors were not all that broken up over the little dog's misfortune. Everyone thought this would finally deter him from chasing everything and everyone in sight and finally it would calm him down. However, it never would. He now chased everything on three legs with a metal support rod around his left back leg that supported a doggie metal cast. After the bone healed, he still chased everything, but with a hop and skip in his get along.

The worst part for the little Beagle dog that had a bloodline to hunt rabbits was of course, not to be able to hunt rabbits when called upon. Max's first trip to the woods was not that successful. In fact, it was a disaster. As we walked through the woods, instead of Max being out in front of me sniffing for a fresh rabbit scent with the older dog Babe, he would not leave my side. As we walked along, a rabbit actually sprang up and started to run away while Max just watched. For the very first time in his life, he discovered something he did not want to chase.

I looked at the dog and just shook my head. Then, I raised my twelve-gauge shotgun and fired at the rabbit. The sound of that blast sent Max on a dead run for parts unknown, and in a second, he was gone from sight. His gimpy leg did not slow him down that much, either. I did not find him until two days later. I had to return to the roads of the area calling his name. The second day, when I returned home and told my mother I could not find him, my dear mother, who loved everyone and had the kindest heart of any person I have ever known, literally jumped for joy and shouted, "Hooray!"

The next day, I was back looking for Max. There he was, jumping up and down with excitement to see me. When I brought him back home, my mother, who I had never heard utter a curse word, was openly unhappy and cursed me for finding the little dog she had grown to dislike so much.

Max was a funny dog and I loved him in spite of his many shortcomings that caused so many people, especially my own loving mother, to dislike him so greatly. My mother could no longer tolerate the little dog and his never-ending and unrelenting attacks on her garments, which was a habit that he would never outgrow.

One day I came home after being away for two days and Max was gone. After two years of putting up with the mischievous little dog, Mom had had all she could stand and his last assault on her dress was his last.

Mom had called the dogcatcher to come and collect Max and to put him away. The dogcatcher knew Max and was not an admirer of the short four-legged car and people chaser, either, and was delighted to do his duty.

The neighbors did not mind seeing Max go either, especially big Billy. I may have been Max's only friend, with the possible exceptions of my brothers Ty and Frank and cousin Jackie De Stevens, who Max didn't feel the need to chase. Jack had become a fan of little Max because Max did make us laugh.

My brothers, Jackie and I would sit on the steps of our front porch and laugh at some of the comical things he would do; especially when he chased big Billy or how infuriated my mom would get after another torn dress compliments of the little dog. People just did not understand the short Beagle. He was not mean or vicious; he was just playing and having fun.

I would not speak to my mother for a week after the dogcatcher took my little friend away. Mom said, "I do not care, Michael. You can be mad at me all you want, but Max had to go and all the neighbors and I are really glad he is gone."

I said, "Yeah, Mom, but now who's going to terrorize the neighbors and give Billy his daily exercise or who is going to rip your dresses and aprons?" After a brief moment, she laughed and so did I. However, it was too late for little Max and his misunderstood behavior.

As the years went by, we would sit on the front porch and always have a laugh over the misunderstood little Beagle who just could not keep out of trouble but could always make me, my brothers and my cousin Jackie laugh.

8 GREAT ADVENTURES AT THE BOATHOUSES

The 1950's was a time of wonderment and discovery living in the Flats of the small town. There was so much to discover and behold, and every day was an exciting adventure. Some of our favorite places were the Boathouses, which were exactly that; they housed personally owned boats on the shores of the lake at the foot of West Fourth Street. These Boathouses would later become Wright's Landing.

The owners of these wonderful retreats had created these for one sole purpose, of this I am sure. They served as a sanctuary from a wife's weekend orders to do this or to do that. This was a man's refuge; a sheltered place where a man and his sons could go to be free from the household chores, like cutting the grass, fixing the fence, a door or anything else not functioning to the perfection of a wife's wishes.

This was a place where a man and his sons could do whatever boys and men loved to do… go boating, fishing, swimming or just relax and do nothing without the interruption or interference of a wife's scolding frown at the sound of gas being released from a beer can or husband.

The boathouses had great characters such as Windy Auclair and his sons Bobby, Larry and little Windy; Walt Pospisle and his boys Joe and Carl; Mr. Muldoon and his sons Bobby, Dickey and Timmy; Mr. Russell and his son Peter; My uncle by marriage Jupe Verdoliva and his sons (as seen below) Ronnie on the left, Kenny, (holding Scratchy the cat) and Michael (holding Trixie the dog).

The boathouse owners would graciously allow our gang to fish from their docks, and from their boats and would even deliver us to the massive ruins of the half sunken barges that were still half out of the water as they rested deep in the muddy bottom just a dozen yards from shore. These deteriorated ruins provided great fishing and we caught large and small mouth black bass, rock duke, jack perch and on the rare special occasion, a Great Northern Pike.

They would also deliver us to the middle of the harbor, the river or the breakwater wall where the water outside the harbor was clear, deep, cool and especially inviting on a hot summer's day.

There was a diving board we built on the half-sunken barges and another that my cousin Ronnie Verdoliva and the Leonard brothers, Ross and Eddie and their gang built at the end of the coal trestle; and yet one more that served as the high diving board at the terminal to the east of the grain elevator.

Jackie De Stevens (left) & Doc Colasurdo at the Terminal.

We would dive from the coal trestle diving board and swim 200 yards to the cable crossings at the breakwater wall where the water was warm, shallow and sandy. We would run across the top of the breakwater wall and leap over the boulders and into the water fifteen feet below.

All along the shoreline of the boathouses during the late afternoon, the barbecues would be fired up to cook their catch of the day, chicken, hot dogs, burgers or a steak. The mouth-watering aromas would fill the air and remind hungry young boys that it was time to make fast tracks for home for the evening meal. It was either that, or face a confrontation with Dad. He insisted on everyone being home for the dinner meal when he took his place at the table.

The boathouses were without debate the greatest place on earth to a young boy brought up in the Flat's.

9 OUR SOAPBOX BUGGY

Just like the defining expressions of the boys in this photo, there was great fun riding soapbox buggies down Van Buren Street hill. It truly was something we loved to do in the summers of our youth.

These small, crude vehicles were soapbox buggies, and they were the source of great fun. Building one was a fun-filled and rewarding group project. Everyone went to work trying to build the fastest soapbox buggy possible, for it was a source of great pride to have the bragging rights of having the fastest soapbox buggy on the steep Van Buren Street hill.

We would use all our resources to get the best materials we could find to build our buggy roadsters. The first place we would go for the wood was right in my backyard, where my Dad had a small stockpile of prime pieces of lumber he stored for special projects.

We would pick out the pieces we wanted and that evening when my father got home from work, we would plead our case to him and beg him to donate the prime pieces of lumber to us for our soapbox buggy.

Dad appreciated a worthy group project and would consent to our choices but not without a list of chores for repayment. Dad believed we should learn the value of working for what we got. We of course agreed to his terms, which were always cleaning the garage or weeding Mom's garden or some such small chore.

The next morning we went to work nailing, drilling and screwing the body of the soapbox buggy soundly together.

Now we needed the most important parts, the wheels and axels. It would take time to locate the perfect ball bearing wheels that were good enough for our soapbox buggy. We searched the neighborhood high and low for the rest of the day and were very sad to find nothing even close to what we would need to be delivered to the bottom of the Van Buren St. hill before all others.

That evening we sat sulking; our long faces down in frustration over our failure to locate the needed wheels and axels for our buggy. My father pulled into the driveway and I was surprised to see him struggling to remove something that looked like junk from the back of his vehicle. After a closer inspection, I could see that it was junk that Dad had salvaged from Sammy Gordon's junkyard. It was a dilapidated old baby carriage, but the axels and wheels were perfectly straight and had the ball bearings that were essential to reach the great speeds necessary to be the champion racers of Van Buren Street hill. My face was glowing with joy. Dad had gotten us the final parts we needed to finish our soapbox buggy and we were as excited and happy as we could possibly be over Dad's thoughtful gift.

The wheels were great and so was my dad. The surprising part was all we had to do in return was promise to be good. We quickly agreed.

He then wanted to help us take the axels and wheels from the junked carriage but we said, "Sorry, Dad, you cannot help us because that is against the soapbox buggy rules." Dad said, "Well, boys, rules are rules," and he left it up to us.

This turned out to be a more difficult task than expected, as the old carriage frame was riveted to the axle. However, with the use of Dad's large workbench, a strong bench vice, a variety of tools and a hacksaw, we would eventually separate the frame from the axle. Blood from our scraped knuckles was lost in the process and there was some bending of the axles. However, Dad's great bench vice was again the answer.

We straightened out the axles and we soon had soundly attached the final and most important pieces to the front two by four and the back two by six of our precious soapbox buggy. The two by four in front was attached to a twelve-inch wide plank in which we had drilled a hole. We then connected them together with a bolt and double nut and washers so it was able to move so that we could steer the buggy to the left and right. We could not have been more thrilled and proud of our new buggy.

The final touch was to open some used paint cans that still had some paint left over inside from painting the backyard fence. We gave the buggy a coat of white paint. The old wood sucked up the paint like a sponge, so we added a second and thicker coat, which we later discovered to have been a mistake.

Mom allowed me to borrow her floor fan that she used to cool her kitchen on the hot summer days after she finished her mopping. I wanted to use the fan to blow air onto the wet paint overnight to help it dry faster. In theory, this was a sound idea. However, in reality, we had put the paint on way too thick. The next day we had white paint on our pants, shirts and legs because the paint needed more time to dry. However, we were in far too much of a hurry in our quest for glory down the Van Buren Street hill to worry over the proper amount of time required for paint to dry.

The following day, we had the new buggy on the top of the steep Van Buren St. hill. My teammates and I sat down on the buggy for its maiden run and we were off down the steep incline at a breakneck speed. We knew, without question, that we would defeat anyone with this magnificent new hot buggy with the less-than-dried paint.

At the bottom of the hill lived the Germaine family and their two young sons, Tommy and Ricky. Tommy, the younger brother, was not yet six years of age. I do not know why, I guess it was just excitement, but he would run dangerously close in front of the speeding buggy as we sped by. Every time, it would scare me because he would run dangerously close to me. This was a serious concern because the speeding buggy and I were moving very quickly and he was only inches away.

The new buggy was a great success, although not much to look at. Sammy Gordon's wheels had given us a great advantage with the choice baby carriage wheels with lubricated ball bearing wheels. We were sure to beat any challenges.

The next day we were back again riding down Van Buren St. hill looking for challengers. However, no other buggies had shown up.

I had yelled at the little Germaine boy several times on my practice runs that morning, as he continually crept dangerously closer and closer to the front of the speeding buggy. His mother had seen him do this and scolded him, demanding that he never do it again, as she shook the little boy by the arm.

Later that day, after lunch, we were back up on Van Buren Street hill. Much to our frustration, there were still no other buggies in sight. How could we bask in soapbox buggy glory if we had no one to defeat? This was not the dream we had envisioned.

On my next run and still without a challenger, I was going very fast. The little Germaine boy once again came running out in front of me. This time I could not avoid hitting him as desperately as I tried. The crash sent the little boy tumbling into the road and I could hear the sound of his leg bone breaking. The sound made me sick to my stomach.

I was familiar with this terrible sound, as I had heard it just a few weeks before. At the West Park playground, there was a young boy that had fallen off the ten-foot high slide at West Park. He landed on his arm and broke it so badly that the bone came through the skin. I had been standing close by and heard and saw the terrible sound and gruesome sight.

I was terrified. I knew the little Germaine boy was badly hurt. As his mother came running across the street to get him, I said, "Oh, Mrs. Germaine, I am so sorry! I am so sorry!" Without hesitation, she said, "I saw the whole thing. Mikey. It was not your fault." As she picked up her son, she repeated, "It wasn't your fault, Mikey." Tommy's mom had warned him more than once.

I still had a sick feeling in my stomach over the sight of the distorted leg of the little boy that now his foot faced the opposite direction like a ventriloquist lap dummy. I was also amazed that the young boy never once cried.

In less than five minutes, my mother had arrived on the scene as the word of the accident shot through the neighborhood hot line. Again, Mrs. Germaine was quick to point out to my mom that the accident had been unavoidable and it was not my fault. In just a few more minutes, the ambulance arrived and sped the little boy and his mom off to the hospital.

The next day, I would sign the little boy's cast that now protected his leg. His mom told me that he never cried until the doctor had to reset the leg, which was surely (as Oswegonians would say) wicked painful. The little boy was now once again smiling as his leg was in a large cast that went up to his knee. That would be the end to any future buggy racing for me on Van Buren St. hill. It was also the last time little Tommy Germaine would run in the road in front of a soapbox buggy.

My dad hung my buggy on the wall of his garage and there it stayed for years. To be honest, I have no recollection as to where that buggy ever went after that. My last memory of it was hanging on my dad's garage wall.

When my father heard the story, he put his arm around my shoulder and said, "Son, sometimes in life bad things happen to good people. It was not your fault, son. Mrs. Germaine has made that perfectly clear over and over." I appreciated his kind words, but from that day on, I vowed to stick to baseball and the Boathouses and never again raced soapbox buggies down Van Buren Street hill.

10 BASEBALL AT CASTLE SCHOOL

On top of the hill at the corner of West Van Buren Street and the corner of Montcalm Street was the grand old Castle School where we first began our educational journey. It was a wonderful old castle style building built in the 1840's, by Fredrick Carrington, who owned an important flourmill. He also owned the Varick Canal, a hydraulic canal supplying water-powered energy to other industrial users.

Fredrick Carrington built the mansion known for generations as "the Castle" or "Carrington's Folly."

This remarkable old structure was the property of the Allen family. Miss Allen agreed to turn the castle into a school for grades one through six for the first ward. Miss Allen was a very short, white-haired, elderly woman. As part of her agreement with the city, she would serve as the principal and first grade teacher. This was part of her negotiations for the home to become a school.

I can tell you from personal experience that the little, white-haired woman was never without her long hickory stick pointer. She was quick to use this across the knuckles of any young boy's hand that she felt was not giving her their complete attention. No first grade boy ever got through her class without experiencing the stinging and painful blow of Miss Allen's hickory stick.

The grand old Castle School was a very special place and everyone who went there was heartbroken when they opened the new Leighton Elementary School near the "Forks of the Road" in 1956. They closed our beloved Castle School and bused us all to the modern new school.

The old castle was a struggle in the winter months. We had to climb a very slippery Van Buren Street hill. However, coming home was much more fun sliding down the hill.

We would now be bused to our new school. We had the greatest bus drivers: Dynamite or his son Murray Gould who bused us to the new Leighton School at Otis Field, which was perhaps two miles away.

Mr. Gould and his son Murray were two wonderful characters and they were great fun to be with as they delivered us safely each day to school and then back to West Park. Many of the children thought Dynamite was a rough old cob because of his deep and rough voice. However, I always knew his bark was worse than his bite. Both he and his son had a great sense of humor and were kind.

In time, I was able to talk Murray into taking a different bus route. My suggestion was to take Liberty Street around to Lake Street and up West 3rd Street to West Park. He could then let our large gang off at West 3rd and Lake St. He smiled and consented to do this, which saved the gang the three-block walk, which we greatly appreciated during the cold winter months.

When I made my proposal to Murray, he just looked at me and shook his balding head, as he knew where I was going with my proposal right from the start. Then he said, "Mikey, you will go far in life," and he then laughed in his unmistakable raspy voice. He patted me on the head as he shook his head in disbelief that such a small boy would have the courage to do what he just did. I would then get a rousing round of applause from the gang for saving them three blocks extra walk each school day.

Murray and his dad Dynamite (who had earned this nickname from his powerful tone of voice) was truly a rough old cob but in reality, he was a kind and gentle man. I loved them both for they were great men and living legends in Oswego during their entire lives.

Dynamite owned the bus service, as well as the horseracing track that later became the Oswego Speedway for popular short dirt track car racing and then for super-modified stock cars. Old Dynamite was at one time the Mayor of the City of Oswego. In my opinion, and that of many others I have no doubt would quickly agree, that these two men were two of Oswego's finest sons of all time.

Dynamite and his son Murray were very successful and they did it while being honest and fair to all. Murray had a raspy voice while Dynamite had a thunderous voice and could be heard yelling to the children on the bus to "settle down" and "get in your seats." The kids that did not know how kind the men really were would shake in their boots.

Although we badly missed Castle School, we loved the bus rides every day to Leighton School and our friends Dynamite and Murray Gould who drove us, especially after we were dropped off right in front of our houses on West Third and Lake Street.

11 DAD'S RULE

1952: The Colasurdo Boys

Frank age 3, Tyrone age 5 and Michael age 6

Our dad was a kind and understanding father who we all greatly loved and admired. My brothers were very well-adjusted, but I was more of the rebellious type and it seemed trouble could find me anytime it looked.

Dad had made rules for us to abide by. These rules were pretty much the same as you would find in any household with young boys and included; don't argue with your mother; obey her; be home on time for the evening meal; do your chores without a fuss; be respectful to others at all times; and only pee in the toilet (unless it was an extreme emergency.) However, there was one rule above all that would make my father furious when broken. His rule was that I was not, under any circumstances whatsoever, to hit my younger brothers.

Since I was the eldest son, it seemed to me that this rule should have been called the Mikey Rule. There was never a mention made of a younger brother striking an older brother. When I questioned my father about this, he said it would not make any sense for a smaller child to strike a larger child.

This would prove to be the only error in judgment I would ever see my father make. This would be a major struggle for me, and by far the hardest challenge for me.

My younger brothers Tyrone and Frank were well-behaved little boys. However, they were well aware of Dad's rule and in a position to take advantage it. As young boys who were holding a get out of jail free card, they were without fear of their older and much larger brother. Whenever they felt the urge to watch my neck swell and my face to become bright red they would torment me. They enjoyed it far too much which made me that much more furious.

Whenever we were out of sight or earshot of our parents, my brothers would push me to the edge just for the enjoyment of knowing they could. Tyrone, who was sixteen months younger than me, would mainly do this verbally by calling me names that he knew would infuriate me. He was the champion of sending me into a rage that would be the cause of my neck swelling and my face to turn beet red. My youngest brother, Frank William, whom I called Willie, was three years and nine months younger than I was and only half my size. Ty, who was a late bloomer as far as growth went, was not much bigger.

Willie was for the most part good with me most of the time. However, he would get in the act on occasion if I rubbed him the wrong way. When he did, young Willie would be much more devious in his actions than our brother Tyrone. Willie would be quick to whack me as hard as he could and never without a solid, hard and heavy object in his hand. That heavy ashtray would inflict immediate pain, and the short little man would run screaming bloody murder into the kitchen and under my mother's apron strings, yelling that I had struck him. This created the definite possibility that my dad might take me over his knee if Mom revealed this story to him later that evening when he arrived home from work.

One day when I was twelve years of age, I was practicing my guitar in the living room, when my little brother Frankie (who was about eight years of age at the time) came into the living room and turned the TV on. He told me to go somewhere else and practice my guitar because he wanted to watch television. I responded by telling him I was there first and for him to get lost. Thus, the verbal war began.

The relatively inexpensive Spanish guitar was a birthday gift from my parents just a year before. Although it was not an expensive guitar, I cherished it and had aspirations of one day becoming a gifted guitarist after I had retired from playing center field for the New York Yankees. While my younger brother and I continued to argue back and forth, I set my guitar down on the couch and went to the other end of the house to use the bathroom.

I returned just a few minutes later. I walked through the dining room before entering the living room, and approached the archway separating the dining room and the living room that at one time years before had had beautiful French doors that folded to either side. From where I was standing in the dining room, I could not see my father's favorite heavily cushioned chair on the right side of the wall where he sat each evening reading the newspaper and unwinding from his long workday. The chair had heavily padded large armrests and it was out of eyesight as I entered the room.

Before I reached that archway, I could see that my guitar was no longer on the living room sofa where I had just moments before left it. This made me fuming mad, for I knew who had moved it.

I yelled, "Willie! Where is my damn guitar?" Just as I walked through the living room archway, standing high upon the armrest of my father's favorite chair out of my view was my little brother. He was holding the neck of the stringed instrument like a baseball bat high over his head. Without notice, and before I saw the short boy that was now sufficiently elevated, he smashed the stringed instrument squarely over my head, shattering my prized guitar into pieces as I went to the floor in shock.

As I was half-dazed and in rapidly increasing pain, he quickly bounced from his perch, threw the busted guitar at me and ran to the kitchen and the shelter of my mother's apron strings. There, he claimed I had struck him with the now shattered stringed instrument.

I bolted after him running into the kitchen like a raging bull. I wanted revenge on the little man. My mother would run interference between the short boy and myself; however, the devious young guitar-wielding boy kept Mom squarely between us out of my grasp. Mom yelled, "Michael! Calm down! Calm down!"

The rule that I had come to despise with all my being came rushing to the forefront of my enraged mind. I suddenly began to calm down. I sadly held the now smashed stringed box that was now only held together by a few dangling guitar strings.

It suddenly occurred to me that being the first-born son held no sway with the woman who had given birth to me. Being the eldest son was not gaining the respect I had hoped it deserved, and was certainly not turning out the way that I hoped it would.

After watching me rub the newly protruding knot on my forehead with one hand and holding the neck of my smashed guitar with the other, my mother began to snicker. Short snorts soon came from her nose as she tried to hold back her emotions. She soon began to laugh, at first in spurts and then in uncontrollable bursts. Soon, her youngest son joined in. Finally, with a vision in my mind of how funny this must have looked, I too could not help but start to laugh as well. Within a moment, we were all laughing uncontrollably.

The more I thought about the actions of my little brother, the more I could not control my laughter. This was unusual, because the little guy was not usually this violent. I guess he just really wanted to watch television.

Now that calmness had prevailed, and order had been restored, it was decided by mom that this story should not be told to my father who was always the protector of the younger boys because I was so much bigger and stronger than they were. Dad would never have believed his youngest son would ever make such an unprovoked assault on his much larger brother. He would never have believed such a thing about the actual way the incident had unfolded and I might have experienced yet another unwelcome cord struck.

That evening, while my brothers and I watched television, I could hear my mother and father laughing uncontrollably in the kitchen and I knew it was not over a joke that Dad had heard at work.

I figured Mom must have told Dad about the guitar incident. Dad may have been somewhat proud of his fearless eight year old's act of bravery. To tell you the truth, I was impressed with his courage, as well. Besides, Dad was not about to punish his baby boy for an act of bravery. Therefore, I just left it alone and I always figured Dad appreciated the fact that I did.

12 THE OLD Y.M.C.A.

During the winter months, we would go to the YMCA on West First St. just across from the Oswego Public High School for athletic activities.

I had always thought this was a very peculiar building. When you first walked up the steps of the entrance it looked just fine, and on the first floor, it was. There were two ping-pong tables or, as the guys that were any good at ping-pong called it, "table tennis" as though that gave the game more dignity and credibility. There was also another pool table. On the second floor, there was a second old pool table, which the better players referred to as "pocket billiards." By whatever name you addressed them, these tables were in use non-stop. To be able to get a game on any of the tables was a time-consuming effort.

The rule was that the winner would play the next numbered challenger in line, so unless you were very good or very lucky, your wait ended after just one short game, but you would be at the end of another very long line before you could play again. Needless to say, it was just not worth the wait. We had suggested to the manager that it would be nice to be able to get a few more tables; however, they always claimed the YMCA had no funds to be able to acquire new, or even used, tables.

Fortunately, Mel Dodge would open Gold Crown Pocket Billiards with about a dozen brand new regulation four and a half by nine-foot tables. After a few years of practice, I would become a better than average player. However, I was never in the same league as the elite players like Kenny Skillen, Walter Knopp, Victor Canale, Mike Verdoliva, Tommy {Banana} Thompson, Billy Rivers or a few others that were all just short of becoming professionals.

I would go on to win a tournament at the Gold Crown years later in my handicap division group, although admittedly there were better players in my group. I was just fortunate on that day.

The upstairs section of the old YMCA was by far the better section of the building. On the lower levels was where the basketball court was located. This was a very small court, and it was enclosed on all four sides by brick walls painted light and dark green. These brick walls were on three sides and were just a foot from the painted boundary lines marking the sidelines of the court. This could be a dangerous place to be when running at full speed. Only on the north side of the court was there room for two lonely benches to sit on; however, they could each only seat three boys upon them at one time.

It was the same deal again. There was always a line of teams waiting to challenge the winner of the current game in progress. Again, if you lost your game, it was another long wait in line before you would get another opportunity to play. However, we were far better at basketball than we were at ping-pong or commanding the cue ball in the early days. Even so, the older and much bigger boys would soon make short work of us.

I can recall one game when we were playing on the matchbox court. I was on a fast break driving towards the basket at full speed. This was always a great challenge for there were loose boards in the old floor. If you bounced the ball on one of the boards as you ran, the ball would not bounce back up to you. Running at full speed with an opponent hot after me, I laid the basketball up for a lay-up just a fraction of a second before I smashed full speed into the brick wall just a foot behind the basket. I hurt all over for a week later and I never played on the YMCA basketball court, pool table or ping-pong table ever again.

This was all very frustrating. However, the worst part of the "Young Man's Christian Association" experience was the swimming pool. This pool area was very small. It was about ten feet wide by fifteen feet long and was surrounded by lime green cement walls and ceiling. A boy five feet tall would have to bend down to avoid a head-on collision with the ceiling when entering the pool. The sides of the pool were just less than five feet from the low ceiling. It had a one-foot ledge between the wall and the pool, and you had to put your back against the wall and sidestep to get around.

The YMCA pool had been built inside an existing small room.

The small room was all cement and was incredibly loud. It was a small echo chamber of deafening sounds that were magnified by all the young boys yelling.

The water had so much chlorine in it that you could still smell it in your nose the next morning, even after another shower at home in the evening before you went to bed. The old YMCA was not that great of an experience. To be truthful, I hated to go there, but I loved to participate in all competitive sports.

The final straw for me with the YMCA came with my most uncomfortable and embarrassing moment that was the worst of my YMCA experiences.

I never understood why you were made to swim naked with a bunch of other boys of all different ages you had never met before. I can honestly tell you that this was an extremely uncomfortable situation for a nine or ten year old boy to encounter.

One day, I was in the pool and in walked a boy maybe three or four years older than I was. I looked at this young man as he entered the pool naked and I could not believe my eyes. I looked away, but this was my first realization that not all boys were created equal. I then quickly removed myself from the YMCA pool area as fast as I could, never to return.

When my mother asked me a week later why I no longer wanted to go to the YMCA and I told her the story, she could not help but laugh, even though she tried to hide it from me. I said, "Mom, you may think that's funny, but believe me, I don't."

Then my mother turned and walked away and I could see she was trying to hold back a burst of laughter as she buried her face in her kitchen apron. I could hear her from another room letting snorts escape her apron as she tried to contain her laughter.

She displayed the same kind of smirk I saw from my mother and her two sisters Eileen and Mary, during the many times they sat at mom's kitchen table having one of their marathon chats that lasted for several days, only to take time outs for sleep.

I was about eight or nine years of age when I walked into the kitchen and began to tell them the story of what had happened when I was on my way home from playing ball at Castle School. On the corner of West 5th and Van Buren St. there was this huge, but very friendly, Great Dane who was taller than me. I knew the dog was very friendly and he was surely big enough to ride. I, who was a big fan of cowboys and horses, tried to mount and ride the large dog. He thought I was playing and got behind me and put his long legs and paws up over my shoulders and around my neck as if he wanted to ride me. I could not get him off me. It was some time later before I understood why my mother and her sisters found such great humor it that story.

I would sometimes sit in the kitchen just to watch all three sisters talking at the same time. All three had the unique ability to change topics of conversation right in the middle of a sentence. It was an amazing thing to watch. I can assure you that they are all sitting at some heavenly table that no longer requires sleep time outs, doing the very same thing right now.

After one of her marathon chats with her sisters, I once asked my mother, "Mom, what is it that you and your sisters talk about for such long periods? She thought for a brief minute and replied, "Oh, nothing." I said, "Mom, please tell me just one thing you three discussed." She looked at me with a blank deer in the headlights sort of look and said, "Oh, nothing in particular." I again repeated the question, "Mom, please tell me one thing you and your sisters talked about... just one." This time she actually stopped and thought about my question. After a few minutes, she laughed and said, "I can't remember." I shook my head and we both laughed.

Then I said, "Mom, when the next marathon conversation starts, begin by asking your sisters what you all discussed the last time you all chatted and see where the conversation goes from there. It should be interesting to see what they can recall, although I doubt they will remember much either." I guess that just goes to show that women just like being with each other. What they talk about does not really matter.

13 THE GREAT DISCOVERIES

Fort Ontario, Oswego New York

One early summer's morning when I was eleven, I was running through the house, excited to get to the ballpark to indulge in a full day of baseball. I was heading for the kitchen door as quickly as I could, but my mother heard my footsteps as I ran through the house. She cut me off at the kitchen door, snatched ahold of me by my shirt and said, "Not today, young man. I have a very important chore for you."

I immediately sent my mind scrambling for the perfect excuse that would set me free from whatever her pressing task might be. However, no matter how I pleaded my case, she would not relent. The short woman of four feet ten inches had a grip on me like Sam Huff of the New York Giants. She would not have any of my excuses or attempts to free myself on this sunny summer morning. She maintained her vice-like grip on my shirt. It became obvious to me that I was doomed to yield to her wishes with no possible chance of escape.

My determined mother informed me in her most serious and convincing tone of voice, "You are not playing baseball today, Michael. You need to dig up the ground in our backyard for a garden that I plan to cultivate." I was to get to it immediately and without any backtalk or excuses, or she would report to my father, who was by all accounts, the enforcer for my mom.

Through careful observation and study of the short woman, I had long since discovered it was never in my best interest to push her past her boiling point. I felt I had developed the skills to talk my mother into just about anything I wanted to do, as long as I did not make her mad. However, this was a new side of her I had never encountered. She had put her foot down and there was nothing in my arsenal I could draw from to change her mind.

It was time to withdraw and accept defeat. I was treading in unknown waters and she had her mind made up. I was afraid to venture any further because a confrontation with the enforcer for not minding my mother would be painful.

Just the night before, my mother made me stand next to her as she washed the dinner dishes. She had given me orders to dry them. I would only be excused when every dish was done. This was an unacceptable task for a boy who was supposed to be outside winning the Whiffle Ball homerun derby that took place every evening directly in front of our house after the dinner meal.

I had been complaining at a feverish pace at the injustice and torment of this undesirable task. I tried to explain to her that this chore was created for daughters. My mother said, "In case you are unaware, you have two younger brothers. If you see a sister, go and get her." My mom had just finished rinsing off her favorite large wooden salad bowl. She was becoming more and more agitated with her complaining son. Finally, she could not take my complaining any longer, and turned and hit me squarely over the head with her very favorite and very heavy wooden salad bowl. It busted cleanly into two equal pieces. Then the woman who had given me birth said, "Oh no! My favorite bowl!" She was clearly more concerned for the wooden object that had just delivered so much pain to her son.

I looked at her in astonished amazement as I rapidly rubbed my head. She then began laughing; at first in short snorts, and then hysterically. In just a few moments, I could not help but laugh at my mother crying and laughing at the same time. It was a funny sight to see my mother with half a salad bowl in each hand. She must have had a sudden feeling of guilt for assaulting her young son and she dismissed me from the dish-drying task. I immediately bolted out of the kitchen before she had a chance to change her mind.

As I ran to join my beloved home run derby competition, my head was throbbing, but I was smiling happily. I was free of her dish-drying towel and figured it was worth the new knot on my head. The next night after the dinner meal I said, "I'd help you with the dishes, Mom, but I don't think you can afford to lose any more of your favorite dishes." She laughed and said, "go on and get out and play." Without hesitation, I was out the door and gone.

After my recent experience with Mom's salad bowl and the new realization that pushing Mom too far would be a very bad idea, and having already made some of my best efforts pleading and begging, I realized I had badly failed. Under great protest, I loaded my father's wheel barrel with hoe, pickax, shovel and rake and headed to the appointed location of her newly found passion.

She marked off the area for me to dig up and spouted off her orders like a Marine Corps Sergeant. This behavior was another side of the short woman I had never before encountered. I began to dig up the sod and soil beneath my feet.

I continued to grumble about this terrible unjust treatment of the next Mickey Mantle. She was detaining me from my destiny and my preparation to get there with an agricultural preparation that had been so rudely thrust upon me without warning or possibility of escape. Seeing no possible chance to get away, I decided to give her one more shot. In my most convincing voice I said, "Mom, you are no farmer and neither am I." I begrudgingly accepted this rude and unjust fate and with pickax in hand, I began to loosen the grass-covered soil. I could see my dear mother desperately trying to hold back laughter as she walked away with her face once again buried in her apron.

After fifteen minutes of unenthusiastically swinging my pickax, I struck something very hard that sent out the sound of metal striking metal. This sound struck a nerve in my spine and my eyes immediately widened in excited curiosity as to what lie just inches beneath my feet. I was now swinging my pickax with far more energy. Much to my great surprise, within just a few minutes, I had uncovered a twelve-pound cannonball.

My curiosity and excitement were now growing at a feverish pace as the imagination of an eleven-year-old boy raced wildly out of control as I now considered the possibilities just below my feet.

My attitude instantly changed. This was no longer an undesirable act of forced labor. This was now an exciting and very desirable "treasure hunt" with very exciting and serious potential. With one cannonball already in hand, I began to ponder what else was to be found in Mom's new garden. I had visions of a pirate's sword, pieces of gold, and a treasure chest. My imagination was now completely out of control and I was digging like a boy that was possessed and driven by an uncontrollable force. Turf and dirt flew with each swing of my trusted pickax.

In the next sixty minutes, I had uncovered two more cannonballs. Within an hour, I had uncovered a total of a half a dozen cannon balls of the six and twelve pound varieties. That was the extent of my findings other than broken glass and ashes that were in abundance in the under turf.

After cleaning the metal objects of destruction with a rag and the water hose, I took some of Dad's 10/20 motor oil from his work bench in the garage that he used for lubricating his lawn mower and tools to prevent them from rusting. I covered the newly found round metal objects with the slippery substance and then wrapped them in old rags from the overflowing ragbag hanging on the wall of our garage conveniently next to Dad's workbench.

As my excitement and curiosity continued to mount at a feverish pace, questions continued to flash to the forefront of my mind: how and why were they there? Had there been wars fought in Oswego centuries before? Fort Ontario was far across the mighty and very wide Oswego River. How were these cannonballs five hundred yards west and two hundred yards south of the shoreline?

By mid-morning, the neighborhood gang had turned up looking for their clean-up hitter who was now long overdue at the ballpark. After sharing my excitement with the gang about this incredible find, my mom appeared to inspect my progress and to make sure I did not disappear. She had heard the gang arrive and she knew I was capable of being talked into escaping her garden task.

Mom was in shock and disbelief over her garden preparation being almost finished in such a very short time. She was equally impressed over the six cannon balls I had dug up from the very same location. However, she was surprised and disappointed to see the underlying dirt filled with ashes and busted glass. Mom said, "You boys should load these cannonballs in your bicycle baskets and take then to Fort Ontario and donate them to the Fort Ontario Museum. They may be able to tell you why the cannonballs were in our backyard."

We collected the now lubricated and heavy round metal objects and wrapped them in rags. We put them in our bicycle baskets and with great excitement, were off to the Fort Ontario Museum at Fort Ontario to seek answers to this newly found treasure trove of previously unknown origin and history.

At the Fort Ontario Museum, we discovered that there had once been a fort where Montcalm Park resided called Fort

George (also nicknamed Fort Rascal) Another, called Fort Oswego, had been located right where our family home now stood, so that is why the cannonballs where there. The west bank Fort Oswego was originally named "Fort Pepperell" and was built originally as a trading post for fur trade with the Iroquois in 1722. It was later fortified into a substantial fort in 1755, which is when the name was changed to Fort Oswego.

In 1756, The French General Montcalm and a force of 5000 French and Indians sailed across Lake Ontario to Oswego from Canada. The General and his troops put all three Oswego forts under siege. A fleet of General Montcalm's French ships sent hundreds of cannonballs raining down on Fort Oswego, where my family home now stood. That fort had been destroyed just a year after it been upgraded to fort status. That was why I had found the metal objects of destruction just inches below the grass in our backyard.

Those cannonballs had been in my family's backyard since August of 1756; some 200 years before when Montcalm's ships had sent them raining down on Fort Oswego.

This was also the beginning of new nightly dreams for a young boy with an out-of-control imagination. I would also daydream of the great wars that had taken place right where I now laid my head at night to sleep. I could see the great French ships as they sent waves of cannonballs crashing into Fort Oswego and the carnage of destruction they delivered.

On the floor of the Fort Ontario Museum there were many similar cannonballs piled high in the shape of pyramids and held in place with one inch by two-inch boards nailed to the wooden plank floor.

Suddenly, my remarkable find did not seem as great as it did just a few hours earlier. Nonetheless, it was still special to find those cannonballs in Mom's would be garden.

On the walls of the Fort Ontario Museum hung several old maps of old Fort Oswego. I could see that Fort Oswego had been constructed approximately where our house was located.

This was an enlightening and amazing discovery for the gang and me. This discovery led to the beginning of many new adventures that would involve tunnels, forts, treasure hunts, and a willing excavation of Mom's garden, which made her very happy.

Dad had taken to using a sifting screen to remove the glass and ash from Mom's garden. It was made of a wire screen nailed to the sides of two 2 x 4 boards. This also made mom happy.

The circle around Fort Oswego is where my parent's home was later located, which ultimately led to my discovery of the cannon balls that had been delivered by air two hundred years before.

We now had a new found interest and thirst for knowledge about the history of the fort that once sat in the very same location where my family home now stood. What other treasures would we discover? Why hadn't our teachers taught us all about the exciting history that actually took place right in our own backyards?

Before leaving the museum, I would donate five of the six cannonballs to the Fort Museum, keeping one six pounder for myself as proof of my story. It was a reminder of my first real life treasure hunt in my own back yard and my newly gained knowledge of my beloved hometown's amazing history.

This was an amazing day in the life of an eleven year old boy that all started because of forced labor and a side of my mother I had never before seen. Nevertheless, it ended with an unexpected treasure I would never forget.

14 THE GRAIN ELEVATOR

The Grain Elevator was just a short distance from our home and we could see it clearly from our sun porch. This mammoth structure stood out on the harbor's shore like a great rectangular cement mountain that was visible from far out in Lake Ontario and for miles along the shoreline.

As young boys, we would go to this very tall structure for collecting baby pigeons not yet capable of flight.

We would climb the towering stairwells to the catwalks half way up inside the very high cement walls to collect the baby pigeons. We were young and it was an extremely steep walk up to where the baby pigeons lay. About one third of the way up, we would physically experience our bodies doing uncontrollable things they had never done before. Our knees were physically knocking and our hands were shaking uncontrollably. It was a very weird and scary sensation for a boy at such a young and tender age.

We would collect the baby pigeons that were in the straw nests built by their parents in between the metal support beams that supported the stairwell and catwalk. We would gather the small birds in a sack and bring them back to our garage in our backyard where my Uncle Bobby Knopp (who lived with us) had turned part of Dad's garage into a large pigeon coop. He had accumulated over one hundred beautiful Fantails, Homing Pigeons and my favorites, the Tumblers.

I was not exactly sure why my dad had allowed my uncle to do this, but it gave all the children in the neighborhood great pleasure to be able to get up close to the beautiful but very skittish birds while they were in the coop.

Each day at 9:00 a.m. and again at 5:00 p.m., our gang would show up in our backyard when my Uncle Bobby would flush the birds from the coop and out into the sky for their daily exercise.

The show of acrobatics these graceful creatures would perform seemed to be in complete harmony, as they would fly in unity in a huge circle overhead.

The tumblers would perform their tumbling acts, flying high, then rolling over, and falling from the sky. This was wonderful to watch as we fantasized about taking flight to join them. Uncle Bobby glowed with the joy of a proud father as he stood with his hands on his hips as he watched his family of birds in flight.

We would lie there in the grass lost in our own desire to soar high above the rooftops. We could never wait for the next flight to take place. Just like clockwork, the birds would come back to the coop, coming in to land like airplanes on an aircraft carrier. They would come swooping down and land on the board outside the porthole Uncle Bobby had provided just for that purpose. Uncle Bobby had cut a hole for them in the top of the garage under the Cornish of the roof. Uncle Bob would be there with a sack of grain he had collected from the piles lying on the ground that was always in abundance at the grain elevator.

I used to think to myself that those birds thought Uncle Bobby was their dad. I think Uncle Bobby was happy in that regard for he truly loved and cherished those birds.

My Uncle Bobby never married and those birds were like his own family. Perhaps that was why my dad allowed him to keep so many. There were strict rules from my father about a complete daily cleaning of the messes they made. Uncle Bob would complete his daily duties faithfully.

My mother had promised her mother on her deathbed that she would always look after Bobby, and she did. No matter what the reason, my mom was loyal to her younger brother and to her promise to her mother. She looked after and took care of the kind and gentle man whom we all loved so much.

Mom never complained about the pigeons and she appreciated the free fertilizer for her garden, plants and rosebushes that she cared for with great affection.

It was an unforgettable sight when my uncle would enter the bird's coop and the birds would flock to him and perch on his head, arms and shoulders. You could see the joy in his face that these wonderful and usually very shy creatures loved him.

Uncle Bobby was a gentle, warm and kind person. One only had to observe him with his birds to understand that. Those shy, skittish creatures would not have given their trust and love to one who was undeserving. He was sincerely a gentle, kind and good man.

RIP Uncle Bobby.

15 SUMMER VACATION AT HATCH LAKE

1957   Dad   Frankie   Mike Tyrone

Every summer for as long as I could remember, we would spend Dad's weeklong summer vacation at his boss' beautiful camp in the Adirondacks. The camp was a knotty pine with four bedrooms, a huge living and dining room with a fireplace, and a kitchen that was a chef's dreams come true. It had a very large yard and it was all fenced in. The large sun porch was enclosed and furnished with comfortable furniture that was heavily cushioned. The large porch extended out over the lake and had a magnificent view.

My brothers and I would waterski every day all day in the big wooden Penn Yan boat. It was truly a magnificent summer vacation camp and we looked forward to it each year.

It was great to see my dad get a chance to rest because he worked six days a week, eleven hours a day to provide the best he could for his family.

Although our home in Oswego was only a few hundred yards from Lake Ontario, Hatch Lake was where we learned to waterski at very young ages. Hatch Lake was very deep and was very cold, even in August when we went on vacation. When you fell from the water skis, you wanted to get back up and out of the water as quickly as possible. Other than the exceptionally cold water, it was paradise and we loved our time there every summer.

16 THE COAL TRESTLE AND THE GREAT FONTANA

There was a never-ending flow of coal cars coming into the Port City of Oswego by rail from the coal mines of Pennsylvania. It was then transported out by ship to destinations throughout the Great Lakes.

This had been going on for about one hundred and fifty years and had earned Oswego the descriptive title of, "where the rails meet the sails." In 1820, when the great wooden vessels of the Great Lakes would come to Oswego to load the coal, they would transport it throughout Northern America.

Long before the coal shakers were built on the coal trestle on the west side of the town of Oswego, there were great log ramps that would elevate the coal cars so the coal could be sent down chutes to load the coal onto the ships. In the 1800's in Oswego, the great coal trestle structures were built from two hundred year old trees that were abundant along the shores of southeastern Lake Ontario and the Oswego River. There were three of these great coal trestles built in Oswego, two on the east side and one on the west.

East Side Coal Trestle

West Side Coal Trestle

There was great demand for coal. The great ships needed it for fuel to move about on the Great Lakes, to be to deliver the soft black shale to ports to heat homes and to fuel the great factories that lined the banks of the Oswego River and factories like them throughout the Great Lakes.

The coal trestle was another place of never ending action and intrigue for young boys of the little city and their wild imaginations.

The coal shakers would replace the great wooden structures of the coal trestles. The long extension arm would feed the ship's bellies with coal. It looked like a monster overlooking the harbor. I would sit high on the top of Lake Street above the boathouses and dream of how great it would be for me to one day be the captain of the great Fontana, sailing the waters of the Great Lakes. I imagined all the exciting adventures I would encounter and the many pirates I might have to outwit.

While I was perched high on this prime elevation that provided a grand view of the harbor, I would look at the massive long arm of the black metal monster that fed the ships the soft black coal. That long black metal arm extended high out over the ships' deep dark caverns where the great metal monster would deposit tons of the black shale that filled the great ship's belly. It also sent bellows of very fine particles of black dust high into the air that would find their way into the homes of Oswego.

Mom and all the other mothers in the neighborhood would be furious. Their homes were only a few hundred yards from that coal shaker and the very fine coal dust that went billowing into the air would find its way through their screened windows and created endless amounts of impossible cleaning for each home. They were extremely unhappy over this and understandably so.

Coal dust also came from the massive coal pile at the steam plant station just a mile and a half away. When the wind blew west to east, which was all of the time, the houses would again be the recipients of the unwanted very fine black coal dust. This forced my mother and the other moms to close all the windows of their homes, which eliminated any cool breezes during the hot summer months. However, closing the windows did not stop the fine coal dust from gaining entrance into the homes.

This dirty black coal dust was most undesirable and eventually the steam plant and the coal trestle would contain the flight of this airborne menace with huge fire hoses that they would use to saturate the piles of coal. This greatly minimized the majority of the microscopic particles from becoming airborne.

They did this by spraying vast amounts of water on the massive mountain of coal at the Steam Station. The bulldozer moved across the top of the mountain of coal to move it into the huge furnaces to heat the water to create the steam that would turn the turbines that would then create the electricity to the homes and factories of the community.

The coal shakers also employed fire hoses and a great vacuum to suck up any airborne particles and contain the dust. I can assure you that this was an accomplishment. Keeping the coal dust from flight was greatly appreciated and applauded by all the mothers of Oswego.

I can remember the joy that the neighborhood mothers displayed as they sat at my mom's kitchen table and expressed their complete utter joy and delight over this wonderful accomplishment. They celebrated by sipping a cool and refreshing Tom Collins my mother had prepared just for the occasion along with some finger sandwiches.

They were very happy and understandably so.

We did not realize it at the time that this airborne coal dust could eventually give you Black Lung and kill you in the very same way it killed so many coal miners throughout the ages.

The coal cars were piled high and overflowing with the large chunks. The coal cars would stop over the deep hoppers that were under the railroad tracks at the coal trestle. The long arm of the metal monster would send the coal into the ship's hatches after the powerful coal shaker shook the cars free from their bounty. The deafening sounds created from the coal shaker were heard throughout the entire city and beyond, day and night. This very same deafening sound would lull me to sleep every evening for as long as I could remember.

Each night, before I drifted off into a deep, sound sleep, I would fantasize that the coal monster that overlooked the harbor like a protective metal creature, would blast long streams of fire at a moment's notice at any evil invaders coming from across the great water to invade our harbor. Those shakers' loud noise was the warning to any foreign intruder that if they entered our harbor without permission, it would be death by fire. That very loud noise that could be heard for miles away was only a few hundred yards from my open screened window. It became my security blanket as I drifted off into a deep sleep, only to be awakened by my mother's voice letting me know it was time to get up and get ready for school.

During the day, the ships would be loaded with the coal that would send the black dust billowing from the ship's deep dark caverns. It was a very eerie sight.

We, who were at all times subject to dares and double dares, would run up the gangway and across the sunbaked fiery hot metal deck of the great ship and throw ourselves over the side and into the water far below.

We wore our black, high-top Ked sneakers when we ran across the ship's deck to leap off into the water below. The metal deck of the Fontana was as hot as Mom's cooking skillet over medium heat. This was a fact and a lesson we had learned the hard way.

It must have been a very funny sight for the ships' mariners to watch the gang attempt to run across the ships' burning hot metal deck. The young invaders would scream as their bare feet were on fire, causing them to turn and retreat down the gangway without a moment's hesitation. We then ran for the nearest place to leap into the cool water to relieve the burning pain self-inflicted through lack of knowledge, previous experience or common sense. However, once was enough and not to be forgotten.

When we ran up the fiery metal deck of the ship to leap into the water, we wore sneakers. The more adventurous daredevils would continue up the ship's ladder and leap from the bow of the mighty ship. That was twice as high and far more dangerous and scary, but others would always applaud the daring act for the great courage to embrace such a dangerous challenge.

I can clearly recall a head first dive I made from the bow of the Fontana when I almost blacked out after my head hit the water with great force from such great height. It was my first and last dive from the Fontana's bow. I can tell you it was a very painful experience and I actually saw stars for the first time in my life from that powerful impact.

When I got out of the water, the top of my forehead was black and blue. I knew when I returned home, I would be questioned. My mother would ask how this bruising had happened. This would not be a time for complete honesty. I hated to lie to Mom, but diving from the Fontana's bow would surely have been a grounding offense. I could not bear this during summer vacation.

When I arrived home, I was prepared to spin a yarn to protect my summer freedom. Mom let out her usual gasp that I had heard many times before. There was the time of the snowball war when someone threw a chunk of ice that struck me in the forehead and the blood came pouring down my face. Another great injury occurred when I fell out of a tree on top of Lake Street bank and sliced my arm open on a protruding nail as I tried to grab for something to help me break my fall. By the time I arrived home, I was soaked in blood. There was another time when I was a toddler, while my father was sweeping out the garage that I stumbled and fell on a smashed Coke bottle. I severed my wrist artery and a fountain of blood spurted from my wrist. I had heard that gasp from the short woman before.

I was prepared when I walked into her kitchen and she looked at me, gasped and said, "Oh My God! How did that happen?" I said, "Not to worry, Mom. It looks much worse than it actually is. I got hit with a hard line drive one hopper that took a real bad hop at the ball park." After her inspection, she said, "Please be more careful." That was the end of that confrontation. My fear of being grounded or suffering the loss of my freedom was now put to rest.

Mom could usually tell when I was making up a story. She knew I was not telling her the truth. She would let it go because the truth would probably cause a problem when explaining it to Dad. Mom never wanted to alarm or get my father upset when he came home from a hard 11-hour day at work with something I should not have been doing to begin with. That was something I truly appreciated about the short woman because Dad did not let punishable offenses go unpunished.

That evening after Mom had conveyed my story to Dad, he, who had been a very good ball player in his youth, said, "That must have been a real nasty hop, son. But, you stayed in front of the ball as I have taught you to do. Don't let this bad hop change that. "

Wow! Here I was being praised for my bruised forehead, that had the truth be known, would have been a grounding offense or even perhaps worthy of yet a few more marks on my backside from Dad's displeasure.

Being the oldest son and somewhat of a rebellious child, my younger brothers got a good first-hand education on what not to do. To be perfectly honest, the belt was more of a motivational piece than an actual instrument of correctional discipline for improper behavior. It did serve its purpose well.

I can only remember Dad reaching for that belt once while we were at the kitchen table eating our supper meal. We three young boys went into panic and emergency scramble mode to evacuate the area as quickly as possible. This caused my father and mother to break out in laughter at our mad dash to vacate the area.

After a few moments when we were sure it was safe, we started laughing and rejoined Mom and Dad at the table but not before we were 100 percent certain it was safe to return. Dad may have found humor in it at the time. However, I can assure you that the three of us were not laughing when he reached for the leather belt that was capable of delivering sharp pain. We were out of there as fast as our little legs would carry us.

After my brothers and I had safely escaped, we could hear our parents laughing in the kitchen. As we stuck our heads around the corner to check and see if Dad was laughing, he signaled to us that it was safe to return.

As we started to laugh insincerely, Dad said he was just kidding. We continued to laugh, not feeling sure of ourselves. We slowly returned to the table where I said, "A good joke would have been better and less stressful, Dad."

We all laughed.

17 THE GREAT WHIFFLE BALL GAMES

At some point in the 1950's a brilliant person took a simple idea and invented plastic balls and bats, simulating the great American pastime of baseball. They called the new game Whiffle Ball. Manufacturers saw the massive potential and mass-produced the plastic balls and bats by the millions. The new game swept over the nation like a storm.

Almost overnight, Whiffle Ball was being played in just about every neighborhood in America. Whiffle Ball became an institution in the American neighborhoods.

Directly in front of our house every evening during the summer months we played Whiffle Ball in the road under the watchful eyes of our parents and the evening streetlights that were not very bright, but did provide enough light to carry our game on past sunset.

These fun and exciting games were played every night and became a summer evening ritual that was always preceded by the Whiffle Ball Home Run Derby, that every kid in the neighborhood took great pride in winning – if the Whiffle Ball Gods would only allow.

Our parents were not particularly crazy about the idea of us playing in the road. However, after pleading our case to Dad who had a weakness for anything involving baseball, he would consent. The parents agreed to allow the games to continue because West 3rd St. was a dead end at Lake Street where we played, and there was very little traffic in our neighborhood in the 50's in the evening at that hour.

There was one condition; our parents would insist upon and that was that at all times there must be car watching guards posted on both ends of the street to yell "CAR TIME" if a vehicle should happen to come into the area. This would be a job for the young girls who you would see at each end of the street effortlessly swinging their Hula Hoops as they watched for oncoming vehicles.

You would always hear everyone moan and complain at the inconsiderate motorist that would drive their automobile into our evening macadam ball field on West 3rd Street, and these unappreciated intrusions would always come at a crucial time in the game.

It was great fun for everyone in the neighborhood, and on all of the front porches there would be the younger boys and girls and the parents rooting us on. It truly did become a neighborhood social event every evening during the warm summer evenings.

Mr. Baker and his large family lived directly across the street on the northeast corner of West 3rd St. Mr. Baker had Diabetes and was down to one leg. He owned a junk yard and he had his sons bring home two sixteen foot metal poles that screwed together and placed a very powerful spotlight on top of it and then hoisted it and its electric cable up and secured it to the side of their house that faced the center of the macadam ball field. When they turned on the power the bright light lit up the field and the street like Yankee Stadium, and we all jumped for joy and thanked Mr. Baker for his kind generosity.

There was no expensive equipment for entertainment in the 50's. We were fine playing with what we had lying around and a plastic ball and bat that my dad provided.

The plastic balls would soon become cracked and too busted up to play with any longer. We would tape them many times until they were just too beaten beyond repair. The next evening when Dad pulled into the driveway after work, he would always have a new one so that the beloved neighborhood nightly games could continue. When Dad would hand me the yellow and blue box that contained the plastic ball, I would look up into his eyes and thank him and he could see just how much that meant to me.

Dad, being a ball player and fine athlete himself in his youth, knew how we loved to play those nightly Whiffle Ball games. Truth be known, I believe he loved watching almost as much as we loved playing the great game every evening. You could even catch him smile, expressing an "Atta-boy" for some exceptional play or hit.

Dad's favorite story to tell us was when he was eighteen in North Syracuse N.Y. where he and his family lived. Dad played for a traveling semi-pro team and one day they went to the Auburn State Prison to play the prison team. Dad would tell the story saying that he had had a very good game making several difficult catches, climbing the fence, catching foul balls and had several big hits driving in crucial runs that would eventually win the game.

Dad would go on to say after the game, the Prison Warden came over to him and put his arm around him, and said, "young man you are a great ball player… I would love to keep you here on my team." Dad would then say he would never go back to play at that or any other correctional facility again, and we would always laugh… and so would he.

The nightly Whiffle Ball games began to draw a crowd of people from not just our block but from all around the neighborhood. Mr. Baker's bright spotlight on that tall pool that lit up the street so brightly had aroused the attention of the neighbors from blocks away and had additionally created an evening social event for the parents. Even some of the girls in the neighborhood would make and sell ice-cold lemonade. The Baker boys brought home a popcorn machine, and they sold bags of popcorn for a nickel.

The occasional cars that would pass by would stop and park out of the way and come to watch the great Whiffle Ball games on our macadam field in the Flats

Our folks would watch our every move from our brightly illuminated sun porch. My parents would rock back and forth on the red and white metal sun porch couch, that Mom called a glider. The glider, as mom referred to it, was a couch. However, it was very comfortable with its thick cushions.

As Mom and Dad sipped their evening ice tea, lemonade or orange/lemonade, they discussed the events of the day, the latest evening news reports, or President Ike's address to the nation. This was all on our new nine 9-inch Strong-Berg Carlson TV screen. Dad had discovered that if you put aluminum foil wrapped around the antennas of the rabbit ears you could get much better reception without the picture being all snowy or flipping over and over. It actually worked.

That little Strong-Berg Carlson TV set in the beautiful wood cabinet was the very first television in the neighborhood. The tiny TV screen had just three channels ABC, NBC and CBS, all of course in black and white. There was a place on the dial for UBC or something like that but we never figured out how to get a TV station on it.

The evening news was always Mom and Dad's highlight, with Walter Cronkite who was the most trusted newsman in America. Dad would turn to his *6:00 PM Evening News Report* at that exact time every evening without fail.

Many of the neighbors would squeeze into our living room whenever Ike would be on to address the nation. It was a wonderful place and time, and our neighbors were like family. Everyone looked after everyone else and it was a great time and place to grow up.

18 THE 9-INCH STRONG-BERG CARLSON TV

On Saturday nights just before 8:00 PM my parents my brothers and I would all take our places in the living room in front of the tiny 9-inch screen of the Strong-Berg Carson TV set that surprisingly did not seem that small to us at the time.

Mom would order a pizza pie about 7:00 p.m. and by 7:20 p.m. Dad would go and pick up the "Deluxe Pizza" that was a really big pie and a six pack of Pepsi 12 oz. cans from Pizza

Villa or Vona's, both of which had great pizza.

Dad, would get back just in time for Mom to serve up the pizza just before *Gunsmoke* came on at 8:00 p.m. The old western stared James Arness as the Marshall Matt Dillon, Dennis Weaver played Chester with his wooden leg and Festus, played by Ken Curtis, were the deputies. Miss Kitty, who was the saloon owner and admirer of Marshal Dillon, was played by Amanda Blake. And Doc Adams was played by Milburn Stone. It was Dad's favorite program and my mom, my brothers and I loved it as well. It was a very well done TV western and when it was over the pizza was long gone.

We loved to watch television!

The TV show *Amos and Andy* was taken off the air because someone felt it was degrading. We just thought it was funny. No one in Oswego, NY was prejudiced because there were no black families in Oswego at all to be prejudiced toward, andwe just never thought like that. In fact, Oswego was noted for the Underground Railroad that assisted slaves in escaping to Canada during the dark and desperate years of slavery.

Other great TV programs were: *The Bickersons, The George Burns and Gracie Allen Show, Hopalong Cassidy, The Roy Rogers Show, The Gene Autry Show,* and the extremely popular game show, *The $64,000 Question.* That program was hosted by Jack Barry, who was later involved in a huge scandal because the answers had been given beforehand to a contestant, Mr. Charles Van Doren. It caused all quiz programs of the day to be canceled and it disillusioned millions of Americans.

Unknown Contestant, Jack Barry and Charles Van Doren

There were also many other fine programs. My personal favorite was Groucho Marx and *You Bet Your Life* with Groucho and his straight man, George Fenneman.

Groucho Marx was my favorite because he was so quick witted and really funny. As so many critics have stated, he was years ahead of his time in comedy.

I remember two of Groucho's shows in particular that I have never forgotten.

In the first, Groucho was interviewing a young man contestant who was a handsome and very athletically built blond- haired young man of about 21 years of age. Groucho asked his name and where he was from. When the young man said "Australia," Groucho asked, "What brought you to America? "

The man said, " I go to the University of Southern California." Groucho then asked, "What is that you do at the university?"

The young man said, "I swim." Groucho asked, "What have you ever achieved at swimming?" The man replied, "Well, Groucho, I won six gold medals at the last Olympics."

Groucho then asked, "That is an amazing accomplishment. To what do you owe to your great success?"

The young man said, "I swim 10 hours a day, 7 days a week, 52 weeks a year. I sleep 12 hours every night. I don't eat meat, I don't smoke, I don't drink and I don't run around with woman."

Without hesitation, Groucho removed his cigar from his mouth and said, "Only one more question young man…all that time you were out there swimming around did you ever think about drowning yourself?"

The audience erupted in laughter.

Another great Groucho interview came with an older male contestant. Groucho asked all the preliminary questions, and discovered that the man had been married for 22 years, had 23 children, and he was still very much in love with his wife.

Groucho said, "23 children in 22 years. You know I love my cigar, too, but I take it out of my mouth once in a while."

Groucho's humor was unmatched.

There were some truly entertaining TV programs back in the day and other than *Gunsmoke* and the westerns there was little violence!

That's something you cannot find today, even with 300 channels.

19 THE JAMES FENIMORE COOPER HOUSE

Just around the corner, one house south of Elmer De Lines corner store on West 2nd Street and West Van Buren St., was the famous and very old James Fenimore Cooper House.

Cooper's duty station was at America's most remote outpost, Oswego, N.Y., and he received a commission in the Navy, from 1808 to 1812. It has been documented that he started doing his very first research for the great novels he would write many years later. However; that may have been some Oswego politician trying to give Oswego more notoriety that it may have actually deserved. Cooper would not write those two great novels for many years later. What is a fact was that *The Last of the Mohicans* and *The Pathfinder* were set in the background of northern New York State.

The house looked just the same in the 1950's as it did in the early 1800's. We didn't know about Mr. Cooper living in this old house in our youth, but we avoided the house like the plague, for it was common knowledge that this old house was haunted by a gang of dangerous pirate ghosts from the early days when the pirates terrorized the ships on Lake Ontario and assumedly all died violent deaths.

As the story went these ghost pirates, could be witnessed on the front porch of this old house any evening of a full moon carrying on at the stroke of the midnight hour. Of course, we never actually saw any of those ghosts because whenever someone suggested a meeting at Elmer's store at the midnight hour of a full moon everyone went to scrambling for an excuse as to why it would be impossible for them to turn up.

Everyone knew none of us were allowed out of the house at that late hour, and would have been bent over our father's knee if we ever were caught out at that hour, but that wasn't the reason no one would turn up. We all knew the real reason; it was the fear of ever having to confront a gang of very dangerous sword-wielding pirate ghosts at the witching hour of midnight when darkness and evil filled the air.

The Cooper House was always exciting to talk about, as our young and wild imaginations could project nightmare images of horror and terror that may have or could have taken place.

We loved adventure but we all knew that some things were just better left alone. Cooper's house was at the top of our list to leave alone and never to mess with.

MICHAEL J. COLASURDO

20 THE GREAT BRIDGE EXPLORATIONS

There were great adventures when we would go exploring the magnificent old bridges and tunnels that required detailed study on a regular basis.

One of my most scary experiences ever was crawling through the piles of deep pigeon dropping no less than three inches thick. That was on the shaky old wood planks of the catwalks under the Bridge Street Bridge in the springtime.

The deafening sounds of the mighty Oswego River roared past just twenty feet below along with the sounds of the cars above speeding across the bridge. There were holes in the road of the deteriorating macadam above my head that allowed the sounds of the cars passing by to be heard.

On this day at this time and this place, I was stricken with the greatest fear I had ever experienced. It was a monumental fear and I made a solemn promise to the great creator that I would never ever return if only I could escape this place just this one time.

This was not a story that I would ever talk about or repeat because if my parents had ever heard that story I would have been locked in my room with no chance of escape until my hair was at least speckled with gray.

It was without question one of the most exciting and scariest experiences of my young life climbing along those old boards of the catwalks under the old Bridge Street Bridge. I never did go back, not for all the double dares in the world. That was a scary place to hang out unless you had wings.

I have never returned.

21 FRANI HENDERSON'S GREAT PINTO

There were many other great adventures; one of my favorites was about the girl from the Forks of the Road. Her name was Frani Henderson and she lived on First Avenue near the Forks of the Road.

Frani would ride her beautiful pinto horse through the streets of the Flats with a gang of kids always running and cheering in tow as her horse galloped along. She would always stop at my house and she would allow me to have a short ride on the magnificent animal because she knew I loved horses – or so I thought. I always felt very privileged because she never allowed anyone else to sit on her horse.

I would later discover that Frani would become my cousin Mike's girlfriend, and that more than likely was influential in her exceptionally kind treatment of me.

The pinto was a majestic animal, which Frani took great pride in and cared for dutifully. If the truth were to be known at that time, I would have given several body parts to own such a wonderful horse.

Frani would eventually sell the horse to my cousin Mike, unbeknownst to me. Cousin Mike would unwisely put the horse in his father's backyard inside the very large fenced-in garden and in just a few days what the horse hadn't eaten, he would trample into the ground. My Uncle made him take the horse back to Frani.

I had not known at the time about my cousin having owned the great pinto or I would have pleaded with my father to let me have the horse. We could have kept him at my father's friends farm who had horses. I would have agreed to any conditions.

My father was very well aware of my great passion for horses and would take me to his friend's farm just outside of town. He would allow me to ride his beautiful chestnut colored horses with white stocking lower legs and white stripes on their faces. They were beautiful horses that put me in mind of the cowboy TV star Gene Autry's great horse Champion.

As the four horses would be grazing out in the pasture, I would whistle very loud. All four horses would look up and then come running. They were all magnificent and I loved going to that farm and riding those beautiful horses.

I would smile and be very proud when my father would say, "I just can't believe that a young boy of your age is so fearless of such big horses."

I would say, "Dad I would live in their barn with them if you would let me."

He would just smile and say, "I have to get it cleared with your mother first." Then he would laugh and say, "But, it is not likely, son."

22 THE COLLEGE STABLES AT FALLBROOK

There was excitement and great thrills horseback riding at the college stables that were owned by Oswego State University. The college riding stables were originally located on top of the hill on Route 104 West just past the forks of the road that would later become the South Athletic Field Sports Facility for SUNY (State University New York) at Oswego.

I discovered this amazing place when I was just ten years old, when visiting my cousin George Knopp who lived a few doors from the Forks of the Road on Seneca Street. This would be a place of wonders for me. I would have goose bumps, and I would be thrilled whenever I arrived there. I would ride my bicycle up the long hill at Route 104 and on the very top of that hill there were the college stables where I would stay for hours on end sitting on top of the corral fence watching the beautiful and graceful horses.

From time to time the head wrangler at the stables, who was a very nice man named Pat, would wave to me to come. He would pick me up and set me on the back of a gentle horse after returning from a ride while he walked the horse around the inside of the corral to be cooled down.

Pat could see and understand my love for horses. He would also allow me into the tack room, a place that was off limits to all but the stable employees.

The tack room was where they kept all the horse equipment. I used to love to go into that room just to smell the leather saddles and bridles that were mounted on their special racks built just for that purpose. One day Pat showed me how to saddle soap the saddles to prevent the leather from drying out and cracking, a chore I loved to do. This room was very large, as it would hold the equipment for all the horses.

I can remember thinking that when I grew up I would have a tack room of my own where I would spend hours saddle soaping all my horses' saddles.

Les, who was Pat's boss and the stable manager, had a library of picture books of all the breeds of horses in his office. Les would allow me to sit for hours in his very old but comfortable heavily cushioned, red leather chair and look at all the wonderful pictures of the horses. As I would dream of someday owning several of the magnificent animals of my own, I dreamed they would multiply and I would one day have many. I would give them the best home and care for them and treat them like my family.

I guess that it was plain to see for Les and Pat that I loved the horses as much as they did when they were my age. I just loved being around the wonderful animals and I felt so good whenever I was at the stables. I can remember the chills I would get watching the college students racing the horses around the track behind the stables.

I believe that Les and Pat may have seen themselves in me when they were my age. Whatever the reason, was I was thankful and extremely happy to be able to be around the horses and their surroundings.

The college would eventually move the riding stables to Fallbrook on the Thompson Road, about five miles away. Years later, I would take my own daughter on summer weekends to ride the magnificent animals.

My little daughter, Angela, who I started taking to the stables when she was just five years of age, loved the horses as much as I did. Her face would always light up whenever I took her there. It was one of our very special places, where we spent great times together with the wonderful horses.

The college stables had many great riding horses. Angela's favorite was an Appaloosa named Pepper, a beautiful speckled horse that was exceptionally gentle and Angela's favorite first choice ride every time.

My favorite horse from the very start way back at the old college stables on top of Route 104 was the Palomino Stallion, Indian Joe. However, I never rode him until I was in my late teens. Indian Joe was a very tall and spirited Palomino Stallion that reminded me of Roy Roger's famous horse, Trigger.

He was the most magnificent horse in the entire stable, and perhaps all of America, as far as I was concerned. Indian Joe was also the fastest horse in the stable. He was magnificent; a light gold color with a white mane, tail, and stocking feet with a narrow white stripe down his face. The stallion had never been gelded and was used for stud, because a Palomino colt was worth far more than any other stable horse. This was why he was never (to my knowledge) let out as a trail horse, and the only one I ever saw ride him was Pat the stable wrangler because he was a very high-spirited stallion.

I can remember being in awe the very first time Pat saddled him up and ran him at full speed around the racetrack behind the stables on 104 West. It was amazing and very exciting to behold because Indian Joe was amazingly fast and he loved the freedom to be able to run as fast as he could.

The great stallion and I would become the best of friends over the following years because I knew the way to his heart. I would first ask Les if I could bring a few apples when I came to the stables to visit, and if I was allowed to give them to Indian Joe myself. I could see that Les was a bit uneasy with this request, however, he would finally agree to allow me to do this for he knew my motivation.

Les said, "Ok, Mikey." However, it would have to be while the horse was in his stable and he or Pat would supervise to show me how to hold the apple so I didn't get my fingers bit.

Several days a week, I would bring the great stallion a small bag of crab apples that were not for human consumption. However, horses loved them. The owners of those trees did not mind me picking them, and I had known the locations of several of these trees for years because over the years we would have crab apple wars. I would also take a handful of sugar cubes from Mom's kitchen cabinet and in time, I was the stallion's favorite visitor and new best friend.

I believe that he even looked for me every day and I rarely disappointed him. After a while, Indian Joe would see me coming with a bag and he would get excited and whinny as much as to say, "It is about time, Mikey." Pat used to kid me by saying: he heard the other horses talking and they were getting jealous.

My attempt to win the great stallion over with gifts of sugar and apples would go on for a couple of summers, and Indian Joe and I would eventually create a solid bond and friendship. Even after the stables moved further away to Fallbrook and I did not go there as often, Indian Joe never forgot the little boy with the sugar cubes and apples.

When I was in my late teens and Indian Joe was still at Fallbrook I had become by then very proficient at horseback riding. One day when I was seventeen, and much to my great surprise, Les asked me if I was ready to ride Indian Joe. I jumped up and yelled, "YES, YES, YES, I am, Les!"

Les told Pat to saddle the golden stallion, however, I was to stay within the confines of the corral. I was ecstatic and extremely proud to be the only one other than Pat (to my knowledge) to ever be allowed to ride the great stallion.

After Les and Pat saw how well the horse performed for me and that I was able to handle the stallion, they agreed that I could take him out for a run around the track behind the stables. Les said, "Only a few times around the track, Mike, and then bring him back."

Wow, what an amazing run that was. I had never been so excited and thrilled in my life and I had never ridden a horse that powerful that could compare with Indian Joe. That would be the one and only time I would ride the great stallion. I would have given anything to have owned that magnificent horse.

The following year, I went off to the Marine Corps. When I returned a few years later, Indian Joe had been sold. I was greatly saddened at the discovery that I would never see my great friend again.

Many years later when I would take my daughter riding at Fallbrook we would always ride gentle trail horses but I never forgot the time I had on the great Palomino stallion.

Pat and Les were also gone by then and it was just never the same for me after the loss of my two equestrian mentors and my favorite horse of all time, the great Palomino, Indian Joe.

WHEN WE HAD IT MADE: GROWING UP IN THE 50's & 60's IN SMALL TOWN AMERICA

23 AN UNFORGETTABLE LESSON

I was once the recipient of one of life's great lessons that was delivered in a very powerful way by my loving father.

Within some of us, there exists struggles, as we are confronted with life's many choices. Some choices can deliver a life of misery and sorrow, while others a life of happiness and fulfillment.

One is the choice that is prompted by evil that is usually stirred by ego, greed, resentment; anger and or jealousy.

The other is the good choice. That is the choice that inspired by joy, peace, love, humility or kindness.

Throughout portions of our lives as we grow, many have experienced portions of this war from within.

I would like to share with you an appropriate story of a great lesson delivered to me by my loving father that left an everlasting impression upon my life.

In the year 1959, I was 13 years old. Without any previous notice on an early Sunday morning, my father stirred me from a sound sleep at 4:30 a.m.

While I was still half asleep, he hurried me along to get dressed, and then loaded me into the Oswego County Cleaners laundry truck (a vehicle he sometimes used from his work place) and we headed west out Route 104 West.

As we left the city limits I asked him in my sleep-deprived state of mind where we were going. He told me we were going to Fair Haven Beach to watch the sunrise and to make a very important discovery.

Still groggy from the unexpected sleep disruption, I continued to question my father about why we were going to Fair Haven Beach to see the sunrise. What were we supposed to discover? He just said, "You will soon understand, my son."

After the twenty-minute drive over the bumpy old road, with the cool morning air blowing in my face, my senses were now almost fully restored. Soon we would arrive at Fair Haven State Park and the beach parking lot. I still had no idea as to why my father had initiated this unscheduled early morning trip or for what its purpose could possibly be.

We then got out of the truck and walked along the sandy beach as the sun was just now coming over the horizon. My father looked down at me and said, " Michael I want you to take a deep breath, look around and tell me exactly what you see."

I looked at him with a puzzled look and then I followed his directions. Still without any idea of where this was going, I took my time scanning the area, paying particular close attention to detail, not wanting to miss any possible clue to this early morning mystery.

My curiosity was now at a peak because I was still baffled as to what we were doing there at this hour. I said, "Well, Dad. I see the sun coming up over the horizon. It is a beautiful sight. I see the barren bluffs on the right, and there is a large body of water with an almost flat surface. I see a few cargo ships far off in the distance, and there are several tall lifeguard chairs sitting on the long sandy beach which we are standing upon."

With that my father reached down and picked up a handful of sand and said, "Michael do you see each of these very tiny grains of sand?" He spoke as gravity demanded they be returned to the ground.

The sand flowed freely between his fingers as he rubbed the tiny grains between his calloused thumb and forefinger. As I looked on, I was still lost in confusion and a lack of understanding.

My father then continued, "Each of these tiny grains of sand could represent a person who has lived a life in this world. There are countless numbers of them on this beach. As you can see, not one of them… not one… is any bigger or better than any other."

WOW! My father was right... I looked up into his eyes and I immediately understood the purpose of this unscheduled early morning journey of discovery and his reasoning behind it.

This was my father's way of pointing out the fact that I was making some very bad choices and my thinking and attitude needed to quickly be adjusted.

It was a powerful lesson and I have never forgotten that early morning ride in the cool air and my father's powerful and painstaking delivery. He was pointing out to me that he was more than concerned about the over-inflated ego I was developing over some minor athletic successes that I had had. This was now seriously prying on his mind, for he knew it was cancerous to the character and future of a young boy.

My father said, "Michael, the difference between self-confidence and unappreciated self-centered ego is self-confidence does not have the need to over use the term 'I' all the time when talking about their own achievements. Egotistical people will use those terms routinely to talk about themselves. Self-confident people do not have the need to talk about the things they can do. They will let other people talk about how well they can do something. "

On our return drive home, the more I continued to think about the efforts that my very wise father had made to make his point so that it had a powerful and lasting effect on me, and the more I realized how important this was for him to impress upon me the seriousness of his message.

The more I thought about this, the more his message was being forever etched into my brain. How much he must have loved me to spend the time and effort so that I truly understood how important his message was.

The thought of my father's message ran over and over in my mind in what felt like a much shorter time than it actually was. We drove along in silence for the twenty-five minutes it took to drive home. As we pulled into our driveway, I looked up at my father and said, "I got it, Dad. I will make big changes in my attitude. Thank you and I will make better choices from this day forward. I promise."

My father would never mention this to me again, nor would he mention it to my mother or my brothers. This was between a father and a son. He was a very special man and we all loved him for everything he was, but mostly for his dedication and love for his family.

Many decades have passed since that early morning drive in the cool morning air, but I remember it like it was yesterday. Every time I think of it, it brings a tear to my eye and a smile to my lips for the blessing that was bestowed upon my brothers and me to have been the sons of such a caring and wonderful man.

MICHAEL J. COLASURDO

24 THE INCREDIBLE BLIZZARD OF '58

In the year of 1958, across the great Lake Ontario came blowing the coldest winter winds that anyone could ever remember. The powerful blizzard winds came barreling down from Canada, and they were devastating as the temperatures plummeted. This winter weather was far colder than the unusual winter weather even for the frozen tundra of Oswego, New York.

When these subzero temperatures coming down out of Canada reached the warmer shores of southeastern Lake Ontario, massive record amounts of snow fell in record-breaking temperatures in record-breaking time.

The winter of 1958 would be a winter to remember. It was 8:30 a.m. on an exceptionally chilly December morning and I was already out the door on my way to the Capital Bowling Alley – just six short city blocks away – for a morning of bowling with friends. The old eight-lane bowling alley was located on the second floor over the paint store on West First Street just north of West Bridge Street.

I arrived just as Mr. Jerry Altamonda Sr., the manager of the Capital Bowling Alley, had just opened the double glass doors that led up the long stairway to the bowling alley's huge doublewide metal door. It had been snowing steadily with larger than usual snowflakes the whole way and it was bitterly cold, but nothing unusual or uncommon for the small town on Lake Ontario. However, it was much colder than usual for December.

As we entered the building, I started chatting away with Mr. Altimonda, asking him questions about baseball. He was an expert on this subject. As he went about his duties, he continued to explain the finer points of the game to me. He was an excellent athlete in his youth and had a son, Jerry Jr., who was a year younger than I. Years later; he and I would play on the Babe Ruth and other All-Star baseball teams together. Jerry Jr. had a younger brother George who was also an all-star athlete and both young boys inherited their skills from their father.

Mr. Altimonda was a very nice man who I had great respect for and I loved to talk baseball with him because he knew the game so well. He gave me great insights on fielding and hitting.

After our discussion of baseball, I began bowling. As the morning progressed, I noticed outside the oversized windows that there was no visibility and the snowflakes were much larger than normal and coming down fast and furious. This again, was not necessarily uncommon or usual when snowing that hard but it would usually subside in an hour or so. This had been going on for over two hours. The snow was piling up and showed no signs of slowing down.

Just before eleven o'clock, I could see that the snow was coming down faster and visibility looking out the large windows of the bowling alley was zero .

Mr. Altimonda had just announced over the PA system that because of the exceptionally heavy snowfall, he would be closing the bowling alley in twenty minutes and all must be out of the building by then.

I had already paid for my bowling games and slipped into my heavy hooded coat, gloves and hat and said good-bye to Mr. Altamonda, who told me not to get sidetracked and to get right home. I promised him I would.

I headed out the big metal door and down the long flight of stairs to the double glass doors that opened inward. The snow by now had already drifted up the doors by about two feet. As I looked at the near zero visibility I knew this was not a normal snow fall and I had best get right home before it got any worse, if that were even possible.

I put my hood on and tightened the strings to keep the blistering winds and snow from my head and most of my face as best I could. Then I wrapped my scarf around my face, mouth and head several times leaving only my eyes exposed.

The scarf would help against the blistering cold and cutting winds. When the temperatures go below zero, the cold air feels like it is burning your lungs when you inhale. I then put my head down and started to plow through the snow that was already at my mid thighs. Fortunately, the snow was light and fluffy due to the extreme cold and dropping temperatures, so I was able to make my way through it, but not without struggle.

As I plowed along in the snow, I thought to myself, I hope this will soon stop. I could feel the temperature getting colder and the snow was getting deeper, making it harder to take each step. My house was six city blocks away. The trip from the bowling alley to my home – under normal conditions – would take me no more than twelve minutes; this was going to take much longer.

As I plowed through the deepening snow, I had to stop every few steps to catch my breath. The blistering cold seemed to be getting more painful in my lungs by the minute. Now as I looked at my watch it was 11:30, I had been struggling in the deepening snow for about thirty minutes already. As near as I could tell in the blinding snowfall, I was about two blocks from my home. Visibility was zero, and I could only tell where I was when I would catch a quick glimpse of a building or some other landmark when the wind would hesitate for a rare moment.

The snow continued to get higher and harder for me to plow through with each stride. My thighs were now burning from stress and the snow was melting on my blue jeans at my thighs from my body heat and adding to the burning sensation. It was becoming very painful. This was the first time I started to consider that I might not be able to make it to my home. However, I would not allow that thought to linger in my mind. No matter how much snow fell or how cold it got I would finish this journey and I would not consider anything else as a possibility.

All of this time I felt myself being confused and disorientated. I was never really sure of where I was. Then, a fresh gust of wind would come, and like the eye of a tornado, it was clear vision and I could clearly see where I was. I was at the corner of West 3rd and Van Buren four houses from my own house. I was elated to get my bearings and know I was just a short way to my home and warmth.

The snow was much harder to plow through than ever, and with every step there was pain. I was now stopping to regain my breath every other stride as the snow was at my waist. Each step was more difficult than the last and I was panting like an overheated puppy. I did not know how much the mercury had dropped, but it was viciously cold and continued to burn my lungs with each breath. I held my scarf and my gloved hand over my nose and mouth and tried to inhale without the burning pain. I refused to stop for more than five or six seconds at a time and I forced myself to continue to fight the snow and cold.

Finally, at last, I arrived at my driveway and could now see my house. I was only about ten yards away from the front door to warmth. I had made it, I had reached my destination.

My mother had been standing in the window, but she could not see out. Mom was very much worried about her oldest son.

Once I finally got to the door, I grabbed the snow shovel that was right there beside it and quickly removed enough snow so I could open it. I swung the door outward and allowed the heat from inside the door to hit me in the face, giving me passage into the warmth of my parents' home.

Mom was ecstatic to see her son home safely and she said, "Oh Michael! I have been so worried, I called the bowling alley and Mr. Altamonda said you had just left around 11:00 o'clock and I have been worried sick!"

I said, "It's ok, Mom, but it was the hardest thing I have ever had to do and I don't ever want to have to do it again. The snow was very deep, but the worst was the blistering cold in my lungs. It was just lucky for me that the snow was so light and fluffy. But it was still very hard to plow through after it got up over my knees and thighs."

Then I looked into the short woman's eyes and said, "Have you and Dad ever considered moving to Florida?" She laughed, but I was dead serious.

Mom helped me to get undressed, and she wrapped me in a blanket in front of the opened door of her oven It sent out waves of heat as I sipped some very hot coco. She rubbed my burning legs to help stimulate my flow of blood. Mom then ran a hot bath for me. After I got my blood flowing more freely, I got in. The warm water burnt my semi-frozen thighs, legs and feet. I went back by the oven for another short while before returning to the tub again now that the water had cooled somewhat.

Mom made me another cup of hot cocoa, a sandwich and some steaming hot Campbell's chicken noodle soup from the can that I particularly liked. After I finished the soup I ate some more of Mom's delicious cookies, still warm from her oven. I then took my blanket and lay down on the living room sofa to watch TV where I soon fell asleep.

Over the next few days, the snow piled up so high on rooftops that people would pay us thirty dollars and more to shovel the mountains of snow off of them for fear they might collapse under the weight of the mounting snow. And there was at least another twelve weeks of winter snow to contend with! I would make a winfall of money over the next few weeks, as did all the other guys in the neighborhood, shoveling snow from the roof tops.

There was a huge three-story house on the northwest corner of West Third and West Schuyler streets. It had an extremely steep tin roof. The owner was offering hundreds of dollars for anyone to get on top of the roof and get the snow to slide off in an avalanche style. I would go to sleep several nights dreaming of how I could get on top of that huge steep roof and slide down it, causing the snow to fall off in an avalanche. Unfortunately, it would be impossible to gain access to its peaks without the assistance of a fire truck's extension ladder. That never stopped me from dreaming about the pot of gold at the end of the avalanche, if I could only make it happen.

We were very fortunate during this time of crisis, for our house had a coal furnace in our cellar that my father had tended to meticulously to keep our house warm and comfortable no matter how far the temperature would drop. Dad said not to worry because the huge coal bin in the cellar had just been filled a few days before so he had plenty of fuel to keep us toasty warm no matter what the mercury dropped down to outside.

It was a good thing because the temperatures outside went to twenty and then thirty degrees below zero and some reports said even colder than that. I don't know exactly how cold it eventually became, but I can tell you there were times when we went out to shovel that the cold air burnt my lungs so painfully that it felt like a hot poker straight from the fire. This caused an immediate about face to return inside. That was life-threatening cold that could not be endured for more than just a short time.

Later we would wrap two heavy scarfs around our faces and mouths to prevent the freezing air from burning our lungs but it did not stop the burning completely it just made it bearable.

My Dad, my brothers, my Uncle Bob and I had shoveled the snow from our driveway several times a day but the snow just kept on coming down. We piled the snow so high we could no longer throw a shovel full to the top of the snow pile.

Soon the city's massive snow blowers went to work to dig the small town out by opening the roads. It was just one-lane paths, and only for walking on so that people could get dug out of their driveways and get to the grocery store to get much needed supplies.

Mom and Dad were now able to make it to the grocery store and got plenty of supplies. Mom's cupboards were again stocked and we were prepared if the snow should continue. Mom said that the grocery stores shelves were becoming depleted of all goods, as people were finally able to reach the stores.

What made this storm so very dangerous was the extreme cold, which froze the water and gas pipes of the homes that were heated with gas. After about a week, the city worked 24/7 to clear the roads so the people could get to the stores.

It was an adventure that lasted only several weeks, but the memories have lasted a lifetime. It was the great blizzard of the winter of 1958.

"It was a winter to remember."

25 ISH – THE SCARIEST DOG IN THE FLATS

In the 50's there were no dog leash laws, and the four-legged canines were free to come and go as they pleased. During this period no one ever gave a second thought to locking their doors, and we never felt at risk of being in harm's way... that was of course with the exception of the Sheldon's dog, Ish.

The trip past the Sheldon's house en route to Elmer De Lines neighborhood corner store at West 2nd and Van Buren Street always required time to gather your courage. If overwhelmed by the obsessive desire for penny candy or a cold Popsicle on a hot summer day, you'd have to make a break for Elmer's door, because you were guaranteed to be confronted by the Sheldon's terrifying dog, Ish.

The middle of the block between West 2nd and West 3rd on Van Buren Street was the demon dog's domain, and any kid entering it had to deal with the fierce-looking and very loud barking Ish. He would come bolting out from behind a bush, under a car or anywhere that concealed him, until you were close enough for him to pounce out when you least expected. Then he would be right in front of your face just inches away, aggressively barking a bark so thunderous you could feel the vibrations in your chest. The slimy white foamy matter that dripped from his large white teeth and mouth would scare you half to death. Ish was a damn scary dog.

I would say to the kids in the neighborhood that the mutt just doggy laughs to himself every time a kid soils his or her underwear. He just loved to scare the crap out of us, and he never failed to miss an opportunity to do it.

No matter how many times Ish had come bolting at you from his hiding places and was on you in a heartbeat, he would still scare you stiff, so stiff your legs would not work.

That was always the basis of the nightmares Ish gave every kid in the neighborhood. You could never run away from him because your legs refused to work, no matter how hard you tried you could not move even one step.

That dog was hated by every kid in the Flats; everyone that is, except for Billy Sheldon, who took great pleasure in watching his dog torment the little kids of the Flats.

Billy Sheldon, who was somewhat strange himself, or at least I always thought he was different, because anyone laughing at little kids scared to death and crying after an assault by the terrifying beast had to be weird. Billy always laughed when Ish terrified a small kid.

I even resorted to going around the block, down Lake Street to West 2nd to cross Van Burn to get to Elmer's, but the loud barking dog would still cut me off before I could made it to the steps of the corner candy store. It was like this canine knew where every kid in the neighborhood was at all times, especially if they had thoughts about Elmer's penny candy on their mind.

I once told Mr. DeLine that if he could somehow get rid of Ish his business would more than triple. Elmer would smile and say, "You're the tenth kid today to tell me that, Mikey."

For many years, Ish sent many a kid home with tears in their eyes and soiled underwear. However, we discovered years later that Ish was just a big and scary looking dog that barked exceptionally loud but never actually bit any kid, or not to my knowledge anyway, except for the time Billy called me to come to his house and Ish chomped on my butt, but never drew blood. Then he doggie laughed when I crapped in my pants.

The dog just loved to terrorize children and he did exactly that every single day. Ish was also the center of all the kids in the Flats' nightmares. He and Billy Gunther's dog, who was another nightmare – but at least he was three blocks away and never interfered with acquiring penny candy.

However, that is another doggie horror story.

26 THE BIG CIRCUS CAME TO TOWN

There was always great excitement when the circus would come to town. They would parade across Bridge Street to announce their arrival, ending up at Otis Field, where they had already set up their massive tent by the old enormous net backstop at the Otis Field baseball diamond. The field housed the cement in-ground dugouts that had no covers for shelter from the elements for the baseball players, and that was a different and very weird sight.

This field was where my cousin Ronnie Verdoleva and his team the Rich Field Aces would play. As a very young boy, cousin Ron would take his tagalong little cousin, and I would watch their every move, especially cousin Ron in left field. I would fantasize about the day I would be big enough to run proudly onto this great field to take my position in center field, just like the great Mickey Mantle, who I would replace in the Yankee outfield in the years to come.

There were some big name circuses that came to Oswego in the 1950's in the dog days of summer. Inside the massive circus tent we would excitedly sit on the wooden plank benches of the stands. They were all but shed of the gray paint that had been applied many tears before and long since worn off by the multitudes of people who sat and walked on them. Over the years they gathered an abundance of splinters of all sizes from being banged around, dried out and aged. These boards would rest on the green metal support frames that would bite you if you moved too quickly.

We ate cotton candy swirled around white paper cones, peanuts in brown paper sacks, boxes of Cracker Jacks, and popcorn stuffed in white waxed paper sacks that became transparent in the spots where the butter touched the inside of the bag.

The vendors would deliver all their wares as they moved ever so quickly through stands of the massive tent that sheltered the three rings in the center. We watched the multiple acts taking place at the very same time. The tent was a city block long, and high enough to cover the high wire acts and of the great trapeze artist who would make us gasp as they tumbled through the air and then fly back to their platform in the sky. We gasped and cheered in delight.

There was the thunderous "boom" from the red, white and blue cannon on the extreme left side of the tent that sent a man into flight across the entire length of the arena into the net under the Flying Guyanas who continued to fly through the air high above.

The elephants and the graceful Arabian horses would prance around the arena in perfect step to the circus band, with their colorful red and yellow uniforms and big hats with blue and yellow feathers. The entire band would sit in front of the stands where we sat intently watching and cheering every acts performance.

There was everyone's favorite: the unbelievable lion and tiger trainer that sent a chill up my spine and caused me to jerk in my seat every time he cracked his mighty whip. It cut through the air so loudly and sharply you would get bit by the bench you sat on as you jumped from the sharp sound. There were so many exciting things happening all at once we didn't know where to look first. However, I would rarely take my eyes off the center big ring because I knew that was where the best acts would be.

Our entire town of thousands of people would turn out for this great event on Saturday evenings. The price was just fifty cents for adults and twenty-five cents for kids twelve and under for two hours of wonderful chills and thrills.

The next morning at the crack of dawn, they would be packed up on their train – gone even faster than they arrived. The only reminders that they had even been there were our memories of the great performances and the empty peanut and popcorn bags, Cracker Jack boxes, waxed soft drink cups and the cone shaped paper holders from the cotton candy that lay scattered all over the ground.

They simply vanished like ghosts in the night heading to the next town to do it all over again.

My friends and I would sit around on the cement sides of the underground dugouts and talk about what an exciting life the circus performers must have traveling the world.

After hanging out around the circus for three days and watching each person who had a multitude of jobs, I thought about how hard they all worked setting up, performing and then packing up in the middle of the night. I thought it must be a very hard life, however, it would no doubt be an exciting adventure and not to be eliminated from my possibilities in the future.

I particularly liked the idea of being a member of the Flying Guyanas on the flying trapeze; but hat guy being shot from the cannon looked like it would be a great thrill to do several times a week. After a long discussion of the possible choices of a circus life, we would pick up the papers in the infield. We then took the field for a game of baseball, which I believed and hoped would be my calling and destiny.

27 MR. AND MRS. MURPHY

There was a very special elderly couple who lived just two and a half blocks south of West Third and Lake Street. Mr. and Mrs. Murphy were a wonderful elderly couple and some of the nicest people you could ever hope to meet.

In the fall of the year when basketball season was in full swing, the Murphy's would turn their powerful flood lights on in their spacious back yard that brightly illuminated the basketball court that was there. The Murphy's son Jimmy, who was grown and had a family of his own, had set it up years before, and it was the best basketball court in the entire town.

The backboard was attached to their immaculately maintained old horse carriage barn that had a hay loft and double doors on the second floor, which Jimmy had painstakingly reinforced to give the backboard a strong and very sound backing. The rim, which was only nine feet high instead of the regulation height of ten feet, was great for short young boys of ages eight to ten. It had a pristine net. It was the best court in all of Oswego.

The Murphy's would graciously allow us to play there in the evenings every fall after the supper meal for two hours from 6:30 p.m. until 8:30 p.m., and no later – no matter what the score or how much we would plead our case. Precisely at 8:30, Mr. Murphy would appear on his very spacious and well maintained back porch and announce, "It's time for all good young boys to go home now. I will see you all tomorrow night, boys."

And immediately, the lights would go out.

Now dejected and with heads down, we would follow his instructions as we walked down the long alleyway alongside his large, well-cared-for, yellow brick home that was surrounded by beautiful gardening with countless colored flowers, now weathered and brown from the cool fall air. Their hedges were at all times perfectly manicured by the old gentleman himself, and they, too, were shedding their small leaves preparing for winter's hibernation. The barn was yellow with green trim, and it looked like a picture out of an old *Better Homes and Garden* magazine from 1880. It was truly a special and beautiful home with exceptionally grand surroundings.

By the time we had arrived at the sidewalk in front of the Murphy's driveway, we were already making plans to resume the last exciting game right where we had left off the following evening. We were once again happy as we proceeded to brag of the evening's great plays and incredible shots at our most cherished friends the Murphy's and their kind and generous permission to access their elite backyard one-basket court that would hold so many wonderful memories of our youth growing up in the Flats of our small but wonderful hometown.

Years later I would drive by the Murphy's home during the

sunset hour, and the wonderful old couple were at their usual places, on their front porch of their beautiful yellow brick home with its large front porch that was always maintained in the most pristine condition. The elderly couple were now well into their golden years, and I was delighted to stop and chat with them about the wonderful nights I had spent in their backyard and how they were so well loved and respected by everyone in the neighborhood.

Mrs. Murphy would smile and say, "Thank you, Michael," and would always insist I have more than one glass of her ice cold orange/lemonade that was always on the table at her side, along with a metal ice container filled with ice to cool her tasty and refreshing drink.

The now silver and blue haired couple would always have a table with several extra glasses for those that might – and usually did – happen to stop by on a warm summer's night. I was always pleased to see that others from the neighborhood would stop by and chat with the elderly couple for they were so kind and had given so much to us when we were young.

It wasn't that anyone was just trying to be nice to the wonderful old man and woman; they were special people and loved by anyone who ever knew them. They were especially pleasant to talk to and people were happy to sit and chat with them. The Murphy's were both educators at the local public high school in their working days and they were very intelligent. They were always willing to help out with a problem, but only if they were asked for their advice. They were as wise as they were kind.

The neighborhood was the greatest place in the entire world to grow up in and the Murphy's were our very special and wonderful friends and cherished by everyone. Whenever I would think about them, even as I write this, a smile comes over my face with my wonderful memories of the gracious old couple, Mr. and Mrs. Murphy.

28 THE ALMOST-GREAT WARLORDS

Top L to R Dennis Berry, Steve Kingsford, Doc Colasurdo, Dick Losurdo.

Bottom L to R George Knopp, Ty Colasurdo and Mr. Style Ronnie Babcock

The city of Oswego sponsored Men's City League Basketball for all age groups. We were in our mid-teens and we had put together a very good team of young gifted athletes. We named our team the "Warlords".

Each player on our team was a very good athlete, ball handler and shooter. For example, there was tall Steven

Kingsford, our dynamic rebounder and defensive player. He would feed the ball off to the more talented shooters after a rebound. He was a very good team player and one of the reasons we were so successful.

My teammates, however, would say that I liked to shoot. This was a kind understatement at best, because I usually shot the ball at the basket whenever it came to me, and rarely passed off to another teammate.

Ronnie Babcock, one of our other gifted players, was very smooth and graceful at all sports. I called him "Mr. Style." He used to kid me about one particular story he loved to tell.

Ron's version of the story goes like this: in one of the Warlord's games, everyone had already scored double figures except for Steven Kingsford, our star defensive player and rebounder – who rarely ever took a shot at the basket. He would always pass the ball off to a teammate.

After we had secured the game, everyone passed the ball off to big Steve so that he, too, might score double figures — everyone except "Doc," (which is what the players called me.). Steve got a pass from Babcock and everyone yelled for him to shoot at the basket. They wanted to see him get at least ten points like everyone else.

Babcock would go on to say that out of nowhere came Doc, who stole the ball from his own teammate and made the basket, leaving Steve and the rest of the Warlords dumbfounded.

Now Ronnie swears by this story, so it is probably true. And if the truth be known, I did like to shoot and score as many points as I could. I may have suppressed this story from my mind, for it would not have been my most flattering and proudest moment. However, it was funny at the time; and according to "Mr. Style" Babcock, it still is.

We had a great time and we won each and every week we played. Babcock's favorite line was, "the Doc likes to shoot." However; it was also true that everyone else got plenty of shots off ,except for Steve Kingsford, but you could count on Steve to be the leading rebounder in the game – every game. That was one of the reasons why we won consistently. Steve was a little taller than most guys our age but he had a great vertical leap, and he usually came down with the basketball when going after a rebound.

About the sixth or seventh game of the season we played a team that on paper we were supposed to whip handily. However, these boys were obsessed with the thought of defeating the Warlords and their fancy uniforms.

This team would practice day and night behind big Sam Felise's house, where his dad had paved the driveway and set up a great basket with floodlights. They would practice until late into the evening every night. They made up in teamwork what they lacked in individual athletic skills and ability. Their overwhelming obsession was to defeat the undefeated Warlords at any and all cost.

They were led by George Gill and his brother, supposedly their best players, along with a very scrappy and quick Chucky Annals, who was actually in my mind, their best athlete. Billy "Wiz" Bradley who got the nickname as a pitcher in little league years earlier, played alongside them. Their big rebounders were Sammy Felise, Ray Haynes and Teddy Gorman. A few others, whose names time has long since chased from my mind, also played on the team.

I don't want to discredit their sports ability. They were a very good team. But we just felt we had much better athletes and would be able to out finesse and outplay them with our superior athletic skills and speed.

From the moment the game started, until the half time buzzer, it was back and forth with the lead. They played good, hard, aggressive defense and foiled many of our attempts at scoring. This was unusual and frustrating for us because we were used to running up big scores against our opponents in the league by half time and putting the game out of reach.

By halftime we were behind by a few points and I was fuming mad to think these guys could compete with what I was sure was a far superior group of athletes.

Their appearance was far less impressive than the well-built and dwell-dressed Warlords, who wore very sharp blue, white and gold satin uniforms we had purchased at Lupe's Sport Shop. These were uniforms that any professional team would have been proud to wear.

I was beside myself that we could be behind these guys. Many of them were overweight and not very fleet afoot – or so I thought. However, here we were trailing on the score board – and I hated to lose, especially to this team that had predicted before the game that they would defeat us. This only infuriated us that much more to think these far less talented athletes could even consider such a ridiculous idea.

The game was being played at Fitzhugh Park School on East Tenth Street where the Fitzhugh Park School gym teacher was in charge of the gym. Several years earlier we were playing at that very same gym when an incident occurred.

I, being very young with an uncontrollable temper, despised the thought of a possible loss. I kicked a chair that went sliding across the gym floor and sent the gym teacher (understandably so) into a rage. He had me at the top of his dislike list ever since that unfortunate event.

So, on this day just a few years later, he was keeping a close eye on the wild boy with the bad temper. He saw me again boiling over with emotions, and for sure he would not tolerate another outburst from the rebellious boy from the west side.

It was obvious and undisputable that I was wrong for losing my composure that day in my youth, and I was embarrassed for kicking the chair, but I was a young boy that got carried away with emotions in a game I badly did not want to lose. But that was no excuse for my over the top and inappropriate assault against a chair.

My chair kicking was something the gym teacher never forgot, and it would come back to haunt me.

On this day, much to the gym teacher's surprise, I kept my cool. I kicked nothing. I didn't even curse in my great frustrations, however, it was a challenge.

The Warlords' game resumed, and George Gill and his teammates played a flawless second half lead by Chucky Annals and George. They played like it was life and death, and they had an excellent game plan that they executed well. They played like they were possessed and would not accept defeat as an option at any cost.

The fact was that we played just as intensely and at a very high level. Even the Doc was passing to the open man! However, we were, at the final buzzer, handed our first defeat by a single point – just as we were about to score the go ahead points in the last second.

This was a very bitter pill for us to swallow, as we had our sights on an undefeated season, and it was shot down in flames. However, swallow the nasty and bitter pill we did. On that day… oh, this is painful to this very day… they were the better team.

In 2015 I was back home in Oswego visiting and I was at the old Oswego Country Club where all my childhood friends play golf, play cards and hang out. At the bar were many of my old friends who were all now potbellied, bald and gray haired. My old Warlord teammate and funny man, "Mr. Style" Ronnie Babcock, was not too potbellied, but he was balding. Ronnie could not wait to point a man I hadn't seen in over five decades, George Gill. And Ronnie could not wait to point him out to me and stir the action with the old story he knew would stir our emotions and would send everyone else in the bar into laughter. Everyone that is, but George and I.

My good friend and old Warlord teammate Style Babcock rejoiced in bringing out the old story of how "the Doc loved to shoot," and how I once stole the ball from my own teammate. Only Ronnie Babcock and his sharp wit could so elegantly bring it back to life with so few words. Ronnie yelled, "The Doc loved to shoot!" and George came back with a one liner of his own, "Yeah, but you guys had nice uniforms!"

Wow! Was that a back-handed dig or was I that much on the defensive with an old man I had not seen in so many decades? That was the only compliment going to cross George's lips on this or any other day regarding his old arch rivals and much hated competitors, the well-dressed Warlords.

Without a moment of thought, my instincts to strike back at George's (what I thought to be a digging left-handed compliment) took over, and I said, "Yeah George, they were great looking uniforms. However, not as great as the athletes who wore them." Babcock and many of the others who knew us, erupted in laughter.

This made George visibly uncomfortable. He was unprepared to go any further into a verbal war after so many, many years. That would be the last word, as nothing more was said between the old men on this day and time at the old country club. However, it provided great laughter for all our old friends at the bar, especially Mr. Style Babcock.

It was a sudden surprise to me, and I am assuming to George as well, how much it still stung after all those years. Harboring such harsh feelings from a young boy's stupid basketball game that took place almost six decades before. It was a shock to me, and I am sure to George as well, that two old men would immediately feel such strong emotions after not seeing each other for more than half a century! Talk about flashbacks of painful childhood memories that could have such an emotional effect... this was something I wasn't ready for and ole Style was in his glory.

I suppose...no, I am sure... that is really pretty sad and foolish for old men to even think like that after so many years. However, upon hearing George's name I was immediately transported back in time to that dark memory of that day at the gym at Fitzhugh Park School. And suddenly, and much to my surprise, the intensity was still there for George and me. I was honestly taken back to that moment and the old emotions that were now surging through me. I was in awe that they could still be that strong after such a very, very long time.

I do believe a shrink might have had an absolute field day with that. Childhood competition can bring out the best and the worst in young boys at times in their desire to be the best, and that can be overwhelming, and as it turns out, very long lasting.

Sometimes the greatest growth challenges we must conquer in our youth are that of preparing to be respectful and compassionate towards others throughout our entire lives.

I will try to remember that the next time we meet, Mr. Gill.

29 MACARTHUR STADIUM WITH THE MICK & WILLIE

This was one exceptionally glorious day in my young life. I was twelve years of age, my brother Tyrone was eleven, and Frankie was age eight. We were riding with our beloved father on our way to MacArthur Stadium in Syracuse thirty-five miles from our home to watch an exhibition game between the Mickey Mantle American League All-Stars and the Willie Mays National League All-Stars. We could not possibly have been more excited!

Chills were running up and down our spines as we got closer to the stadium, the home of the Yankees AAA farm team, the Syracuse Chiefs. Dad was brought up on Lodi Street in Syracuse, just a few miles from MacArthur Stadium. He had grown up watching the Chiefs, and had dreams of playing for them one day.

This would be the greatest day in our young lives, going to a live game with the great Mickey Mantle and Willie Mays! To actually watch close up and in person the greatest baseball players in the world, and my personal hero, "The Mick."

The stadium only had ten thousand seats. That meant every seat had a great view, up close and personal to the field and the players.

As we took our seats just behind the American League All-Stars dugout, you could see the goosebumps on our arms. Dad had gotten us some of the very best seats that were up close to our heroes. Even my father was all smiles and glowing, just like his sons on this day. Dad was a great baseball and New York Yankees fan all his life. This game brought back many of his own wonderful childhood memories of watching Babe Ruth at Yankee Stadium in his youth and as a young man in the 1920's. And now here he was in 1958 with his three boys watching the baseball elite not thirty feet away from us.

The weather was very dark and overcast, and it looked like an outburst of rain was inevitable at any moment. However, by some miracle and grace of the baseball gods, it never rained more than a light sprinkle a few times. The darkness of the clouds did, however, ruin the many, many photos we had taken. Those non-developed photos greatly saddened us when the film came back. Only a few photos came out and the other one hundred plus did not.

Before the game there was the great homerun derby between Mickey and Willie, and what a show they put on! The sounds of the balls cracking off their bats rang out so loudly that each one sent a chill up my spine. They were amazingly loud and crisp.

Mickey hit one ball over the centerfield fence that towered high above the flag pole. I almost completely lost sight of it as it continued to climb and soared far over the centerfield wall. It was a tremendous blast off the great power hitter's bat and the sound and the flight was something I would never forget.

I would meet the great Mickey Mantle many years later after his playing days were over, and I told him of that day and that particular home run and he said he remembered it. That was amazing to me because The Mick hit tape measure home runs routinely. In fact he twice came 18 inches from being the only man to ever hit a ball over the roof of old Yankee Stadium.

Mantle's longest recorded tape measure drive was measured at 565 feet. Any power hitter throughout the history of baseball would be proud to take claim to smashing a home run one hundred feet less at 465 feet.

Mickey Mantle was the greatest power hitting switch hitter of all time – and they didn't even know what steroids were back in the day. He had the strength of a lumberjack and the grace of a gazelle. He was nothing but natural power and grace. When Mickey came to the plate to bat every eye in the stadium was on him. Even the vendors would stop to watch the greatest power hitter that ever lived, to see what prodigious blast and deafening sound would come from his mighty bat.

In my opinion, Mickey Mantle was the greatest player to ever play the game – and here I was watching him, just thirty feet away from the grass he walked on.

We were eating hot dogs, peanuts, popcorn and drinking coke from waxed cups. I thought to myself… "This surely must be what heaven is like," as I basked in this unforgettable day with my number one hero… my dad…and my beloved two younger brothers…"Yes this unquestionably must be exactly what heaven is truly like."

After the game while we were making the hour drive back home we would talk (all at the same time) over and over of the great players and plays we had just witnessed on this day, and how we had the greatest father and son day ever, thanks to the very best father in the entire world!

My father smiled with true and genuine happiness over the absolute joy he was able to give to his sons! It was the greatest day ever in the impressionable lives of the three young boys, and I do believe it was equally great for my dad, who no doubt had many flashbacks of his own youth on this day.

Without question I would remember this unforgettable day for as long as I lived. Thank you, Dad for the best day of our life!

Your proud sons: Mike, Ty and Frank.

30 LITTLE LEAGUE, WHERE DREAMS CAME TRUE

In the 1950's every young boy from the age of eight and up had a dream of magically one day becoming the next Mickey Mantle.

"Little League" was a magical place where I and a city full of young Baby Boomer boys wanted to be athletes. Boys from ages eight to twelve had their greatest childhood thrills playing Little league Baseball on the hallowed grounds of Fort Ontario playing Little League baseball.

In the summer of 1958 I was twelve years of age and just about to play my very first year of Little League baseball. I had been trying to make Little League for the past three years. However, I had lost in the large field of over 500 other kids competing to make the rosters of just eight Little League teams. I was finally able to join the Little League team sponsored by the Elks Club.

I was about to have my greatest dream come true. I will never outlive the memories of the great excitement that the baseball gods bestowed upon me under the sun at the Little League Stadium at Fort Ontario, especially the memories of the loud crack of the bat that sent the ball sailing high over the outfield wall and into the bleachers of the Little League Stadium.

The absolute joy and thrill of a young boy hitting a baseball over the Little League fence is hard to describe. I can only tell you that it was an exhilarating feeling that left me with the feeling that I was walking on air. It was a feeling of disbelief, joy, pride, excitement and a tingling all over all at the very same moment and the definite beginning of something new and very exciting in my life.

The very first home run I would hit came against hard throwing Bobby Perkins who was himself the home run king of Little League that year. In 1958 he smashed six long drives far over the right field fence, as the left handed power hitter was strong and graceful and would put you in mind of the great Mickey Mantle himself.

My greatest thrill of all took place a week later on a late afternoon in the midst of summer when we played my brother Tyrone's team, a very good and very well-coached Knights of Columbus (K of C) ball club.

I envied my younger brother for being able to play for such a well-coached team that had great players. They had Joey Sereno who hit four home runs that year, Mike (Cooley) Cloonan, who was an outstanding ball player and athlete, my brother Ty (Rookie) Colasurdo, Tommy (Peanut) Vona, and Jimmy Bevacqua (better known as Buckwheat – a nickname he got as a young boy because he was Italian and in the summer sun he would get very dark colored skin looking like Buckwheat from *Our Gang*.)

Every player on their team was an above average little leaguer. They had Rocko Manicci and Honey Sherwood who were their coach and manager – and they knew the game. They were committed and would practice every night, even when they did not have a game. That practice showed up in their game time performance, as they never made a mental error and rarely made a physical one. Up until that point the K of C had been undefeated, and justifiably so.

In this crucial game my teammate and cousin George Knopp, who was amongst the elite talented Little Leaguers, got a hit in front of me my first time at bat. As the Little League gods saw fit, I would crush a towering home run that sailed far over the left field fence and bleachers, as well as my brother Tyrone's head, since he was playing left field.

On my next at bat, the game was tied and again my cousin George had reached first base safely in front of me. The manager of the K of C changed pitchers, and on his first delivery to me I sent another ball over my brother's head and the left field wall once again. That delivered the only loss the K of C would suffer that season, and truth be known, ,my brother has never forgiven me.

It was a wondrous moment in my life that I still love to relive in my mind. It took place in what at times seems to have been another lifetime ago. It was a young boy's greatest dream come true, and I was blessed by the grace of the Little League baseball gods to be able to have that wonderful experience and memory under the sun at Fort Ontario Little League Stadium in the summer of 1958.

That summer, the K of C had their revenge the next time we met. Joey Sereno, the hardest throwing pitcher in Little League hit me in the wrist in my first plate appearance with his very first pitch. I had the baseball's stich marks in my wrist that entire summer.

Joey also smashed the longest homerun I ever saw at Fort Ontario Little League Stadium.

In center field there were two flagpoles that were perhaps thirty feet high, and Joey crushed a ball that sailed high and far over those flag poles. The sound of that ball hitting his bat was incredible, and that was all Joey needed as he would pitch a shutout against us and would avenge their only loss that little league season.

After the game Joey and I, who were friends, were shaking hands and he said to me laughingly, "It's hard to hit home runs from first base, ain't it?" I just shook my head understanding his message.

Then I said, "Yeah, Joey, but a walk on four pitches would have worked for me without the pain."

I never got mad because that was baseball and a part of the game, and Joey was a very tough kid and competitor. He wasn't going to allow me to beat him with any home runs while he was on the mound pitching, and truth be known, no one ever hit a home run off Joey Sereno's fastball anyway.

Joey and I would be teammates later that year on the Little League All-Stars and again in a few years on the Babe Ruth League All-Stars where we came up just one game short of playing for the New York State Babe Ruth League Championship in a crushing loss in thirteen innings.

31 AFTER LITTLE LEAGUE CAME BABE RUTH LEAGUE

Ty and Doc Colasurdo 1960

In 1960, my brother Tyrone and I would be united for the first time on the same team in organized baseball, the Rotary baseball club in the Babe Ruth League.

This was wonderful for our parents, who could now root for their sons on the same team. They would no longer have to be torn in the middle of the battles when we were on different teams. This was something that greatly pleased them.

It would be my second year and Tyrone's rookie year, which he would bear that nickname (Rookie) for many years to follow. The nickname was given to him by our cousin George (Mate) Knopp, who was my Little League teammate. However, Mate now played for the rival Lions Club, and as I had said before, was an exceptionally good athlete.

The first year I played on the Rotary Club team there were the classic battles with an excellent Lions Club team, featuring great pitching duels. We had the "Great One" Richey Pelow, who was without question the very best baseball player I had ever played with, and arguably one of the very best to ever come out of Oswego, N.Y. He was a five tool baseball player who hit often and with tremendous power. And he was a dynamic pitcher with a blazing fastball and devastating hard slider, which in those days we just called a hard curve. He played a brilliant shortstop when not pitching, and he was fleet afoot. He was fun to watch play the game we all loved so much.

The equally talented Lions Club team had blazing fastball pitcher, Dick Hall, who was later signed to a major league baseball contract while in college. Both teams had better than average players at every position, and when the two teams squared off, there were classic battles, usually ending in a score of 1 to 0 or 2 to 1, with each pitcher striking out 18 or 20 hitters in a regulation seven inning game.

There were other very good teams and players in the Babe Ruth League like the Steelworks' fireball pitcher, Billy

Steinburg; and The Kiwanis Club's Jimmy Biancavilla, who pitched with me when I pitched for the Oswego High School Varsity two years later. We both enjoyed great success as did our team under legendary coach David E. Powers, who delivered championship teams for decades to the Oswego Public High School.

They were all great years growing up and playing America's -- and my own personal -- beloved pastime.

MICHAEL J. COLASURDO

32 WATER SKIING ON LAKE ONTARIO

Living just a few hundred yards from Lake Ontario, we had a speed boat for summer boating. It was mostly used for water skiing.

My brothers and I loved water skiing and had become very proficient on water skis from young ages. I had learned how to ski when I was just eight years old, and I mentored my younger brothers who would both become excellent skiers.

I had first learned to water ski when we would vacation each summer at my dad's boss' camp on Hatch Lake in the Adirondack Mountains. It was a beautiful and very elegant knotty pine camp with several spacious bedrooms and a huge living room with a fireplace that took up the great majority of one of the walls. It was a spectacular place with a huge porch that was enclosed and sat on the water's edge hanging over the lake.

The beautiful camp even had a large fenced-in yard in which we could have a Whiffle Ball home run derby each late afternoon, as the tall pine trees prevented the balls from leaving the fenced-in yard.

At the invitation of Mr. Bonsack, the owner of the Oswego County Cleaners where my father was the General Manager, we vacationed there for a week each summer for as long as I can remember. At the camp, Mr. Bonsack owned a grand old twenty foot Penn Yan wood power boat that was very heavy. It had only a twenty-five horse outboard engine that was sluggish to start because of the weight of the craft and the small horse powered engine. When pulling a skier from the water, the boat struggled to pull the skier out. However; after it got going full speed, it was fine to ski behind. I would teach my younger brothers to sit at the end of the boat dock so it was less drag on the heavy boat and small motor, and they performed very well.

That was where we first learned to ski. When you learn to water ski behind a heavy and slow craft, it becomes much easier to ski when you get behind a lighter more powerful and faster boat. We learned that the hard way initially. However; it would pay off in later years when we could ski behind our own light and much faster power boat.

When I was in my teens, Mom purchased a sixteen foot fiberglass speed boat powered by a fifty horse Mercury outboard motor. It was very powerful, light, fast and great for pulling skiers. We would fly across the waters of Lake Ontario everyday all day during the warm summer months.

I was older and in my late teens. My youngest brother Frankie was now mid-teens, and you could see him and his three inseparable buddies water skiing all day long. They all became excellent water and snow skiers.

Of course, their greatest task everyday was to find ways to fill the gas tank. Somehow, someway they never failed to manage to find ways to support their gas needs. Mom contributed far more than she would have probably liked, and I was working and was always happy to help them.

To support their gas needs, they would do chores to raise the needed money. They could never wait to get in the boat and on the skis.

Frankie would ski all day long with his three inseparable buddies Freddy Casteldo, Bobby (Weasel) Weaver and Spencer (Spenny) McNamara. They would all become excellent skiers, however, not without some bumps, cuts, scrapes and bruises. They would receive these practicing things I would show them, like cutting close to a buoy on one ski or seeing how close they could ski to the breakwall or ending a ski run landing on shore to get off the ski without getting wet. However, they never failed to achieve command of those unusual and dangerous tricks on water skis.

One afternoon when I was twenty, I went down to Wright's Landing, as the four boys were just pulling into the dock. They asked if I wanted to ski, and I said yes. I was wearing a sport coat and tie because I had just come from a wedding reception at the Chart Room, located on the river.

My young brother Frank yelled to me, "Let's go – get in the boat. I have one of your swimsuits here in the boat."

I said, "No thanks," as I was bending over to roll up my pant legs, still wearing the shirt, tie and coat. I said, "I'll just start from the ramp where they put the boats in the water."

The ramp itself was covered with small black cinders; this was something new for the three young boys in the boat. As they laughed at the unusual way to start skiing from land that they had not seen before, they threw me the tow line as I stepped into the boots of the skis.

I then directed them to go full throttle on the gas and off we went. I slid immediately across the top of the water from the cinder ramp and we were off, as the boys and all the bystanders laughed at the skier in a sport coat, tie and pants in too much of a hurry to disrobe.

As soon as we had enough speed, not far from shore, I released one ski and skied on the one ski that had two foot boots, sending up rooster tails 10 to 12 feet high, as I leaned sharply to the side carving my ski into the water with every turn.

As we rounded the coal trestle and made a couple of circles out by the breakwater wall, I continued to lean far to the sides, throwing up the huge rooster tails of water from beneath the single ski. I cut sharply in front of buoys, and the kids sitting on the break wall, and one of my roaster tails splashed them. They laughed, wanting another refreshing spray. We gladly accommodated the young boys, while Frankie and his friends laughed at the antics of Frank's older brother.

After a trip up the river to circle the Chart Room Restaurant where the wedding reception was still going on, I waved at the people I had just been with. They were now sitting outside the restaurant and laughing at the well-dressed skier. I signaled the boys in the boat to circle back close to the Wright's Landing dock where we had first started.

When they circled back around in front of the dock, I was on the far side of the boat from the landing ramp. I cut swiftly across the wake as the powerful speed boat turned, doubling my speed. That was sufficient to get me to dry land. After crossing the inside wake of the boat, I let go of the tow line. I shot across the water and then quickly slowed as I neared the cinder ramp. There I stepped out of the ski boot and onto the ramp. I had timed the distance and speed perfectly, and without ever getting in the water or my clothes wet. To the rousing applause of the bystanders at the landing and the boys in the boat, they laughed and patted each other on the back, shaking their heads in amazement and disbelief.

Once again on land, I rolled down my still dry pants, put on my socks and shoes, and I left, returning to the reception at the Chart Room, where my friends just laughed at my unusual mounting and dismounting of water skis.

A few hours later that day, I would come back to my mother's house only to find Frank and his friends already home, much to my surprise.

Frank's skiing buddy Spenney McNamara was all scraped raw and imbedded with tiny black cinders from his head to his toes. I looked at him and gasped and said, "What the hell happened to you, Spenney? "

Frank and all the boys all began to laugh, as Frank replied, "He tried to do what you did and had way too much speed. He went tumbling head over heels up the cinder ramp."

All four boys burst into laughter at the sight. They could not get out of their minds the picture of their friend going head over heels into the sharp black cinders. He spent months after that, removing them from under his skin.

Those boys were something else, and like I have said many times before, they could find the humor in anything and everything including Spenney's painful crash and burn in the cinders.

The four of them, including Spenney, kept on laughing about it as they gave me the complete details of the event. They just could not stop laughing at the sight that had been imbedded permanently in their minds: Spenney's tumble in the cinder-covered ramp.

Spenney himself kept laughing with them and I don't know how, because he was in bad shape. In my opinion, he should have gone to the Emergency Room at the hospital, but he refused to let me take him. Every time I think of this story it still brings a cringing smile to my face. They could always find the humor in even the worst situations.

Oh how I loved those young, good-looking rough and tumble young boys who feared nothing. I adored them so much.

They were my pride and joy, and each time I see them we always come back to this story, and a few snow skiing stories that are equally as funny. Oh my, the wonderful times I had with those fantastic young boys who all grew up to be great fathers and family men as well as great snow and water skiers.

33 KPS AND JR. HIGH SCHOOL

After completing the sixth grade at Leighton Elementary School, we then went to Kingsford Park School (KPS) Junior High School for grade seven thru nine. KPS was a real joy, for we now changed classrooms every 45 minutes instead of sitting at the same desk in the same room the entire school day – and a whole new social program developed in the hallways.

There were the school baseball and basketball teams that I was eager and excited to join. These were wonderful, organized teams playing in organized school leagues where I would bask in the competition and glory of school athletics.

The KPS freshman basketball team would play the Oswego High School freshman team at our home basketball court, where my cousin George Knopp and I led the team.

This would prove to be a remarkable game for me personally, as the basketball gods were with me on that day. Everything I shot at the basket went in. I could not miss a shot from anywhere on the court. I scored 34 points in the first half, putting the game out of reach.

This was a good opportunity for our Coach Canale to give the second team players an opportunity to play – and he did. Coach did not play me the entire second half. Everyone on our team was very thrilled and happy to have been able to participate in the game, and we went on to win.

It wasn't until after the game that I found out that my teammate and cousin, George's older brother Patrick, held the school record with 36 points in a game. Patrick was an exceptionally good athlete from our family and a personal hero of mine. I ended that game having scored those 34 points in the first half, so my cousin Pat retained the school record for most points scored in a game.

I admit that at first I was somewhat shocked to find this out. If Pat hadn't been my hero cousin, I would have been unhappy with the coach's decision, a decision that would keep me from the KPS record books. However, I never really got mad because Pat was a great athlete and I admired him. I figured I would always be able to have a laugh with him over this. Besides, there were more games to be played with more opportunities. But I would never again challenge the 36 point school record.

One of my fondest memories I have of KPS were the games of bombardment we played during gym class. There were several bombardment balls we played with, and the smaller baseball-sized balls could be thrown very fast by the guys with the stronger arms.

The guys on my team would always throw the smaller-sized balls to me because I could throw them very fast. The other teams would give them to Joey Sereno or Teddy Gorman, who also threw very fast, and at close range you just couldn't get out of the way fast enough. Smaller framed boys like Tommy Vona or Billy Kosteroski, who I must have missed a hundred times during a school year, were the exception. They were able to escape.

If one of these strong-armed boys struck you, it stung and it would knock you down. However, the sight of that brought on great laughter and applause from every boy in the gym. After the initial gasp from everyone, that is.

Bombardment was everyone's favorite game, and when the gym teacher Matt Barkley announced bombardment would be the gym activity for the day everyone erupted with applause and yells of joy. When I look back, I can see we were rather sadistic kids.

MICHAEL J. COLASURDO

34 ICE SKATING AT THE KPS RINK

In the winter there were the evening trips after dinner to Kingsford Park School (KPS) to the outdoor ice skating rink. The rink was a distance of about two miles from my home at West 3rd and Lake St. We loved to go ice-skating in the winter, and our greatest joy was the whips that sent many a boy and girl head over heels tumbling to a snow covered end in the ice rinks surrounding snow banks.

We would join hands and make a long line of at least a dozen kids for a whip. The person at the end of the whip would pick up great speed as we circled, and he or she would be sent flying uncontrollably at breakneck speeds into the snow banks surrounding the ice rink.

This was great fun, as we would whip kids into the snow banks. It was amazing that in all that time and all those whips, not once did any kid ever become seriously injured.

About every forty minutes, we would skate over to the little pavilion where we changed our shoes and skates to try to get our feet warm. The little building was heated by a an old potbellied stove that would give off great amounts of very hot heat. The large blocks of wood burning inside that made the old metal stove red hot. Kids would put their gloves and mittens on top of the stove, and it would send steam up from the melted snow from the garments on the hot metal.

We did get warmer, especially if you were lucky enough to get a seat on the bench close to the stove. My two younger brothers never wanted to go ice skating at the KPS rink because when I told them about the cold and painful walk home, they wanted nothing to do with it. However, they would always have their homework done and I would not.

By 8:30 p.m., we would return for the final time in the little pavilion to once again crowd around the potbellied stove. We changed from our skates to our street shoes and boots. They felt strange after being on ice skates for hours. We made the long journey that seemed much, much longer in the now much colder air. The temperatures had dropped substantially in the evening, and this made for an unpleasant journey home.

We, of course, were dead tired from so many whips, and many times Dad would turn up to pick us up – which we greatly applauded and appreciated. We would always arrive home by our curfew hour of 9:00 p.m. After a cup or two of hot chocolate with baby marshmallows, along with some of Mom's fresh baked cookies still hot from her oven, we were sent into a hot bath. From there, it was off to bed where I would be asleep in minutes, dreaming of the great times we had whipping at the KPS ice skating rink.

35 FRIDAYS MEANT CAHILL'S FISH DINNER

In the 50's and 60's it was Cahill's Fish Market for our Friday night fish dinner. Cahill's had great seafood. It was the busiest place in town each and every Friday before the supper hour.

In those days, Catholics, who made up a large percentage of the people in Oswego, could not eat meat on Friday, so consequently, fish was usually the meal of choice for many families.

This was a religious rule that we never complained about too much because Cahill's had the best haddock in the world, along with a great tartar sauce, French fries, scallops, deep fried clams, onion rings and so much more.

Cahill's also offered shrimp and lobster, which they of course did not get from Lake Ontario. They imported it in from the coast of Maine.

Many times, while I sat on the shore of the west river bank watching the strange looking Cahill fishing boat come in from an early morning fishing trip far out in Lake Ontario, I would wonder how they went about catching all those fish? How many did they catch in a day?

They never ran out of the delicious fish to sell, no matter how many customers they would serve. At least to my knowledge, they never ran out.

There were many times I would worry about that very thing, because there was always a line outside that was always at least a block long. It seemed like it might take forever to get inside the building with the crooked wall.

I would always think that surely, by the time I would finally arrive at the counter to place my order, they would be out of everything. Then, Dad and I would have to go out to Rudy's for our fish – if it were in the summer months and Rudy's was open. However, every time Dad and I arrived at the counter, they were never out of anything. I guess that is why they were in business for so many decades. They knew how to prepare and they could serve the customers at an unbelievable rate of speed.

You could smell the fresh fried fish from blocks away. By the time you got to the door, your mouth would be watering with the overwhelming aroma of deep fried fish that poured from the oldest building in Oswego with the crooked stone block walls that looked like it could collapse at any moment.

Inside was a fine-tuned machine that served customers within a few minutes and people would exit the door with their big white bags of seafood and a content look upon their faces.

Cahill's, just like Rudy's, had an assembly line with people preparing the food for immediate delivery. They had a team that battered the fish, shrimp, scallops, clams, mushrooms and onion rings. A line of seasoned deep fry specialists worked at each station, and each cook had several deep fryers splashing in and out of the hot oil at all times. They knew exactly what they were doing down to the very second that the fish would be cooked to perfection. They sold delicious fish by the tonnage and salespeople moved swiftly, never missing an order or making an error. And by the time you got home with Cahill's seafood, it was all still steaming hot.

Dad was a meat and potato or pasta kind of guy, but he never complained about anything we ever got from Cahill's Fish Market. Mom would always serve it with her wonderful homemade mac and cheese. It was the absolute best you would ever eat!

Dad said Cahill's and Rudy's deep fried food was always lightly golden and so good because they changed their cooking oil frequently. Dad also said that he had heard that Mr. Cahill would filter the cooking oil, and mix it with diesel fuel that would power his fishing boat while greatly cutting his fuel cost.

Cahill's Fishing Boat, the Eleanor D

That was a great idea. Great food and a lower fuel cost However, as Dad said, it was only third party hearsay.

As I look back, I can't understand why we only got Cahill's delicious fish on Fridays, because they were open all week and my mother really loved haddock sandwiches with that delicious Cahill's tartar sauce. I guess the answer to that was Rudy's on the lake at least during the summer months.

36 RUDY'S MILLION DOLLAR HOT DOG STAND

Rudy's Humble Beginning

Dad would also take us to Rudy's on the lake for dinner several times throughout the summer. After we finished eating our dinner at Rudy's, we would skip flat stones on the lake. Back in our car, Dad would continue to drive west around the loop and we would stop at the little soft ice cream stand located on the corner of Lake Road on Route 104.

We enjoyed those wonderful evenings with our family and the food that was always exciting and memorable.

Rudy's humble million-dollar-a-year shack is a very famous and historical local business that thrives to this very day. It shows signs that it will be on the southeastern shore of Lake Ontario for many more years to come.

Its popularity with the people of Oswego and surrounding areas has never declined, and seems that it only gets stronger each summer.

There was a funny story told about Rudy that circulated years ago. Right after he would close his hot dog stand in the fall, he and his wife would get in their Cadillac and head for Florida for the winter.

In Florida, people would ask Rudy what he did for a living. He would just smile and say I have a million dollar hot dog stand back in Oswego, New York on the southeastern shore of Lake Ontario. People would just laugh and say with a raised eye brow, "You have a million dollar hot dog stand, Rudy?"

Rudy's would produce substantial income for decades. It shows no signs of slowing down.

Rudy, and his son-in-law, Brad, have long since passed away. However, you can bet they are both looking down and smiling from the great beyond at the great success their little hot dog stand now enjoys.

It all started so long ago at the small, humble hot dog stand Rudy built just west of Oswego, New York on the southeastern shore of the Great Lake Ontario.

MICHAEL J. COLASURDO

37 THE TEXAS HOT CHALLENGE

In 1963 two of my high school friends, Alan Waters and Danny Donahue got to arguing over who could eat the greatest number of Texas Hots at Rudy's. After Alan claimed he could eat ten of the delicious but very large and spicy dogs smothered in hot sauce and raw onions, the debate was over, and Danny was quick to challenge Alan on his boast. The wager was ten dollars, the time frame was one hour, and Alan could not vomit or leave the table.

The rules were laid out later that day at Rudy's with a crowd of high school friends and onlookers present. Alan went to town, consuming one after another until the ten Texas Hot dogs had disappeared and all within less than the allotted time.

Then, Alan added insult to injury by ordering and consuming two more Texas Hot's and a fish sandwich, cleaning the plate once again just to add an exclamation mark, because he surely could not have still been hungry after that enormous amount of food. This was incredible to watch. Danny not only lost the ten- dollar bet, but also had to pay for the ten Texas Hot's as a stipulation of the bet. He was not happy.

Danny tried to conceal his displeasure, but the redness of his face uncovered his true emotions. He was fuming mad, and at one point during his frustration I thought Danny, who was a hot headed tough kid, was very close to punching Alan in his now extremely bloated stomach. However, if he did, Alan would have surely become a volcano of spent Texas Hot's all over Danny, and that would have added even greater insult to injury.

Danny realized that Alan had made a statement, backed it up and won the bet, fair and square. However, Danny was still mad as hell because he had just lost what was in those days was a huge amount of money, especially for a high school teenager. He also understood that he now had to keep his composure and accept this loss like a gentleman. Nonetheless, it was a very bitter pill for Danny to swallow and it was obvious to the rest of us that Danny was in a huge battle with himself to keep from erupting.

Not Danny, nor I, or any of our gang watching would have believed skinny Alan Waters would have been able to consume all ten Texas Hot's smothered with raw onions and chili sauce. The only thing left to eat was the bill… and begrudgingly Danny Donahue did.

It was an amazing thing to watch and no one would have ever believed skinny Alan Waters could have eaten that much food at one time, considering the fact that Alan only weighed about 150 pounds and had a high school boy's waist of perhaps thirty-two inches. It was a remarkable achievement that provided great entertainment and laughter for everyone there... everyone but Danny, that is.

Alan's stomach was a sight to see as he raised his shirt. It looked like Paul Newman's after he ate the 50 hard-boiled eggs in that great movie of the time, "Cool Hand Luke." It was an amazing day when Alan Waters consumed a dozen Texas Hot's and a fish sandwich to wash it all down and added insult to injury to Danny Donahue and his much lighter wallet.

38 OSWEGO LEGEND – COACH DAVID E. POWERS

My very first encounter with the legendary coach David E. Powers was for me a very memorable meeting. In 1958, when I was twelve years old, we played sandlot baseball every day at our home field of West Park. We would on occasion travel to other sandlots such as Otis Field at the Forks of the Road where my cousin George "Mate" Knopp and his gang played every day, and the Diamond Match Field on the corner of Lake Street and Ontario Street on the west side where Mike "Cooley" Cloonan and his gang played.

All of these sandlot baseball fields throughout the city were in very rough condition, as the infield dirt was hard as a rock and full of holes, with some very deep. However, we rarely complained unless someone misplayed a ball they probably should have caught. They would be quick to say it was because of the rough ground, and many times it was. We also had to be careful not to turn an ankle when running, which would turn you into a non-mobile "umpire" for the rest of the summer – and that would be a horrible fate for a young boy.

Each sandlot gang never had enough players to field two full nine-man teams, so on occasion we would go to another sandlot park and have a game with the regulars at their field.

This was the case on a bright summer's morning when our West Park gang visited the Diamond Match ball field just half a dozen city blocks away. Much to our surprise and great disappointment, there was no one there playing, so we did just what we would always do at our home field and started our own pickup game, as we called them.

The Diamond Match field was surrounded by Ontario Street on the east, or along the third base line. Left and Center field were contained by Bronson Street. On the corner of Ontario and Bronson St., there was a large white house that was set off the road. It had a huge, second story double-sized picture window facing the ball field that also provided a grand view of Lake Ontario. This lake view from the picture window was no doubt the intent of the people when they built the house for its excellent view of the beautiful Lake Ontario sunsets.

Legendary Oswego High School Varsity Baseball Coach David E. Powers was in charge of overseeing the recreation of the parks throughout Oswego during the summer. Coach Powers just happened to be at the Diamond Match field in the children's playground section that offered slides, carousels, monkey bars, sand box, swings and the usual activities for young children you would find in a park playground. This section of the park was located at the end of the right field line of the baseball field on the Lake Street side of the park.

I was not aware that the legendary coach was watching us play when I crushed a ball that sailed far over the road in left field and shattered that huge picture window. Coach Powers had witnessed the flight of the baseball.

Without hesitation, I started running for all I was worth down Lake Street with bat and glove in hand for fear my parents would have to pay for the great window if I were caught. I would be grounded indefinitely for the deed, a thought I could not bear to even consider. That was a very expensive window now shattered into a million tiny pieces. I was responsible for this disaster and I was scared and nervous as to what my fate might be if (or when) I was caught.

As I ran as fast as I possibly could east on Lake Street toward the sanctuary of my home just over the hill on West Third Street, Coach Powers suddenly pulled up alongside me in his car as I ran. He began to shout in his unforgettable voice that would break up so badly when he tried to yell that you could hardly hear what he was saying. "Stop! I want to talk to you! Stop running! I want to know who hit that ball! Stop running, young man!"

Controlled by fear and an overload of adrenalin, I continued to run as fast as my legs would carry me. The coach finally yelled, "Stop running, young man! You are not in trouble! The city has insurance and will pay for that window! You are not in any trouble! You have my word!"

With my adrenaline flooding through me like a raging river and my heart about to pound right out of my chest, my mind raced in fear. Was this just a ploy to stop this chase and capture me? Reluctantly and full of fear, I stopped running and looked into the coach's eyes for any sign that might expose dishonesty. I continued to pray this was not just a ploy to get me to stop running.

Coach Powers got out of his automobile and said, "Come here, young man. I promise you that you are not in any trouble." He reached out to put his arm around me and again assured me the city's insurance would pay for the now shattered window.

He then asked me my name, my age, where I lived and who my parents were. Then he asked me what position I liked to play the best. He began to tell me what a tremendously struck baseball that was for a boy my age.

WOW... talk about mixed emotions. This was an incredible turn of events; the legendary coach who was worshiped by all far and wide was now praising me for an act I was sure would be the cause of the loss of my freedom, a thought that I just could not bear during our short summer vacation from school.

I had to play baseball everyday all day for as long as the weather allowed. I would surely die if I was confined to the limits of the four walls of my bedroom should I be grounded for depositing a baseball through an expensive window. Then Coach Powers told me to get in his car and he drove me home.

As I exited his car, I could not believe the feeling of pride I was overwhelmed with when the legendary coach said to me, "Michael, you will be sure to go out for high school sports when you get to high school. I want you to play for me on the varsity team."

Wow, again! Did he really say that? Did this really happen or was this just another one of my incredible glory dreams that I enjoyed so many nights? Then the great coach said, "I will be looking for you." Then, as suddenly as the whole turn of events started, it ended as he drove off.

When I walked into Mom's kitchen, my mother and her two sisters were sitting at her kitchen table chatting away as they often did. As I walked to the table to sit down still with a dazed look of disbelief on my face, mother said, "What happened to you?

I said, "You wouldn't believe it if I told you, Mom. Your son was just driven home by Mr. David E. Powers himself and he told me he wanted me to play for him on the OHS Varsity."

Mom then said to her sisters, "He has a huge imagination."

I said, "I told you wouldn't believe me."

That was my very first encounter with the legendary coach. My second encounter came four years later at the age of sixteen, when I would try out for the varsity baseball team. Coach Powers was still the coach of the varsity baseball team and true to his word, he had not forgotten the young boy he had chased up Lake Street four years earlier. He was quick to welcome me to the team.

It was unknown to us at the time that this would be the final year of his career. It would be a season of great achievements for our team. One that only the great coach with his superior knowledge of the game and skills to mentor could have developed me into the absolute best player I could possibly become.

Our team that season would crush most of our competition. We only suffered one loss, which unfortunately came during the league championship game. Our defeat came at the hands of the best high school pitcher in New York State that year, whose name was Dick Robarge. He was from Pulaski and he was seeking revenge for the only game he had ever lost in high school, to our Oswego High School team earlier that season.

That season, Coach Powers would recruit another baseball legend in Oswego, Mr. Michael McCrobie. He was born and raised in Oswego and played professional baseball. He personally assisted me with developing sound pitching mechanics.

I was a rough, wild, hard-throwing pitcher. Under Mr. McCrobie and Coach Power's tutelage, I was able to deliver my best performances, with five wins and no losses that season.

To be honest, I could have never accomplished the wonderful things I did that year without the benefit of those two great mentors. Coach Powers would insist I run daily for hours to build up my endurance, and Mr. McCrobie taught me about the proper mechanics of the pitching motion to deliver consistency. They molded me into the very best I could possibly be and for that I was and remain eternally grateful.

My greatest moment in the sun that year came when we played the great Dick Robarge from Pulaski during the season. I struck out eighteen of the twenty-two batters. That was one more than the minimal number of twenty-one batters. To achieve a perfect game in a shutout against the most coveted high school pitcher – who was being looked at by major league scouts – would have been a major coup.

Robarge, the big, left-handed pitcher from Pulaski would sign a professional baseball contract with the Cleveland Indians Major League team at the end of that school year at eighteen years of age.

On this day, we would defeat Pulaski and the great Robarge, 4 – 0. The hard-throwing pitcher struggled with command of his pitches, and we managed a few timely hits after walks were issued by the hard throwing left-hander. On this glorious day in the sun, I was at my absolute best and had my finest hour as a high school pitcher.

We won the game and gave the great high school pitcher Robarge the only loss he would suffer in two years of varsity baseball. The baseball gods were most definitely with the OHS Buccaneers on that bright and sunny day that will be forever entrenched in my mind and heart.

This was the number one greatest moment in my life in high school athletics. Playing for and being molded into the best player I could be by the legendary Coach David E. Powers and Mr. Michael McCrobie, was nothing less than a blessing.

Robarge would have his opportunity to seek the revenge for his only loss a month later. He would not be denied. He delivered a dominating performance, striking out eighteen of twenty-two batters and shutting us out in the league championship game 4 - 0.

In that championship game, Coach Powers would struggle with his choice for his starting pitcher, because I had had such great success against Robarge during the season. However, Jimmy Biancavilla was the ace of the staff and he was a senior and a very good pitcher. Coach Powers justifiably elected to start Jimmy Biancavilla for this championship game.

On this day, the blazing fastball of Dick Robarge would hit its mark time and time again and young Mr. Robarge got the revenge he so badly wanted.

After this game, Coach Powers would walk with me and put his arm around me as we walked away from the ball field for the final time.

He whispered in my ear, "Maybe I should have started you today."

I looked into the old coach's eyes that time had wrinkled and I said, "No, Sir. You made the best choice. Jimmy is a great pitcher and no one could have beaten Robarge today."

Then I said, "But I really appreciate you saying that to me, Mr. Powers. I truly loved being able to play baseball for you."

I cannot put into words strongly enough the admiration and respect I held for Mr. Powers and Mr. McCrobie. They have both been gone for a long time, but neither will ever be forgotten.

The 1963 picture of me that appeared in The Palladium Times when I pitched a no-hitter for the Oswego Varsity Baseball Team

39 OSWEGO HIGH SCHOOL VARSITY FOOTBALL

1963 Oswego High School Varsity Football Team

We loved baseball; it was our passion. However, we would soon discover we also loved football.

I suppose we just loved to compete physically. It was great to release all of the built up teenage aggression that came about as our hormones ran wild with illusions of our invincibility.

Whatever the reasons were, we loved football season and banging into each other without any repercussions from our parents for being physically aggressive towards each other. It was just great fun and we had such great times even through the sore muscles and even some broken bones.

I was excited at the opportunity to finally be able to put a hit on my brother without any repercussions from my dad. The one thing that would upset my father faster than anything was just the thought of brothers fighting amongst each other. That was highly forbidden in our house. I had lived under my father's rule of never strike your younger brother. Breaking that rule would be cause to suffer the consequences of my father's displeasure. I guess it was because Dad never had a brother, and wished he had because he had five older sisters and they were always quick to strike the younger brother if he did not conform to their wishes. Whatever his reasoning was, he made it crystal clear there would not be any hostilities allowed between his sons.

Football was a loophole to Dad's rule. To have physical contact with my brother was allowed on the football field and you can be sure that my brother Tyrone had visions of being able to bang into me at his first opportunity, as well.

I had an advantage because I was physically bigger and faster. However, whatever my brother lacked in physical size and speed, he more than made up for with desire and heart.

He was a fierce competitor and he feared nothing and could

not tolerate losing at anything and I loved and respected him for that because I had the very same feelings myself.

Lovigng, competitive brothers: Me (L) age 4, Tyrone (R) age 2 1/2

Ray Haynes & Ty Colarsudo

The two linemen Ty Colasurdo and Ray Haynes were very good athletes and they played very well together, rarely missing any blocking assignment. One day during a full contact scrimmage Ty and some of the first team offensive line were moved to the defensive side of the ball. I was now running behind a much less talented second team offensive line.

The quarterback called a play that had me running right up the middle on a delayed draw. That play, called a trap, or a sucker play, is run when the offensive linemen intentionally miss their blocks and the defensive player then has an open field to the Quarterback and his lone blocker in the backfield. The QB slips the ball to the running back (me), and while the linemen are pursuing the QB, the running back runs for a gain.

Now, this play works fine if the defense falls for it and goes after the quarterback. However, if they do not fall for the trap, the running back is usually painfully stopped in his tracks by more than one tackler. This happened to be one of my favorite plays because I would be in an upright position when I was handed the ball and I could see everything. Therefore, I could pick my area to run. I could see everything as it unfolded in front of me, and once I would get through the initial rush of the linemen I could run for a big gain or a touchdown.

At the time, I was somewhat aware of the fact that our linemen were a bit upset because I was getting all the write-ups on the sports page. They, who were doing all the hard work, were rarely mentioned. They decided it would be a good lesson for me to learn how much harder it is to score touchdowns without blocking.

Everyone on our team was aware of what was about to happen but me. When the QB came back and then handed the ball off to me, there in front of me was the entire defensive line and not a blocker between myself and them. I was immediately crushed and smothered under the entire line. As they one by one slowly got off of the pile on top of me, they all laughed. I just smiled as they high fived and limped away.

On game day, I would score several touchdowns behind their blocking. Truth be known, our line was exceptionally good at opening holes for me to run through, which they did consistently. Then, I just had to beat a linebacker and or a defensive back.

Besides the talents of my brother as a guard and Ray Haynes the center, we had a very good left tackle, Joe Saltamachia. Running off tackle behind him led to many touchdowns. In fact, that play produced touchdowns in every game we ever played. The boys on our line were very good. We had great fun and the boys really didn't care that much about the sports page stuff, other than the fact our team won. They just liked to have fun and bust my chops or joke around. As I have said many times before, the boys of Oswego could always find humor in anything we did.

40 ENTER "BA" AND SOME BROKEN BONES

One Tuesday there was an afternoon varsity football full contact practice, following a Saturday game in which I had suffered a broken nose. The only thing the doctor could do was place a piece of tape across the bridge of my nose.

I was playing on offense, and my buddy Bobby Axtell ("BA") a fierce football competitor, was a lineman. He also played both sides of the ball on offense and defense. At this particular time, he was playing on defense and I was on offense.

BA had suffered a broken left hand a few weeks before and was playing with a cast that went up almost to his elbow. He considered that cast to be an added weapon because of its hardness.

BA and I were the best of friends and we hung out together all the time. However, on the football field, we were fierce competitors who as naive teenagers thought we were both invincible on the football field.

During this scrimmage, I was running the ball on offense when I ran a play up the middle. I was tackled by several guys, and BA was on top of me while I was on my back on the ground. BA then pushed my face guard up exposing my face and popped my broken nose with his casted hand breaking the unhealed cartilage again. He thought that was a funny thing for him to do. It hurt like hell and I would never let him know that, but I vowed I would get even.

Back in the huddle, I told the quarterback to run the same play again. I then told the center and the guard to double team BA and cut block him meaning one hit high and the other took out his legs. As the football gods of justice and fair play would have it, equaling matters out ol' BA was knocked flat on his back. His casted hand lay flat on ground before me completely exposed. Everything was now in slow motion in my mind. I saw the exposed cast and I stomped on it with the heal of my one inch long football cleats shattering BA's cast. Ole BA, as much as he would have loved to, could not conceal his agonizing pain.

Coach Dilts who watched both of the fiascos blew his whistle and said, "Will you guys knock it off and save the aggressions for the game?"

When you get right down to it, we grew up in the greatest time in history and in one of the best little towns in America. We had loving parents that did their absolute best to instill within us character, integrity, confidence and respect for others.

We grew up strong, confident, happy and without the luxuries of technology or even sports equipment other than a ball, glove and a bat that my dad provided. Few other kids in the neighborhood were as fortunate as us.

As we grew older and participated in high school sports, we were thrilled to have the quality sports equipment furnished by our schools. We wore it with great pride.

In the 1950s and 60's, we did not lock our doors, as there was no crime in the Flats of Oswego, or in the entire town for that matter. There were no computers; the schools had few overweight children because we were active, as we were on the run from sun up to sun down.

We did physical things like climbing trees, riding bicycles, playing sports and games of physical activity. We swam and ran and in the gym, and we played bombardment, which was a favorite.

In the winter, we would slide down hills and then walk back up to the top of big hill to slide down time and again. We went ice skating. We built snow castles and so did our neighbors across the street. We had snowball wars that lasted as long as it took for the last person to be struck and the winner of the war to be determined.

We went sledding and tobogganing at Fall Brook, the country club and down Van Buren street hill. We just went outside and found ways to have fun. Even the children who were somewhat overweight were not obese and had (what I hope they would agree were) affectionate nicknames like Chubby, Moose or Bear. It was a grand place and time and we had a wonderful childhood filled with laughter. For that, we were truly grateful.

There was nothing greater than to grow up in a small town in the 50's and 60's. It was the greatest time in all of history. It was post war, a new industrial age was exploding and we were free to do as we pleased... within, of course, our parent's guidelines and rules.

It was the greatest time and place in all of history to be young and we lived it.

41 THE GREAT ROCK AND ROLL BANDS

Billy and the Barons

Billy Cooke top left, Gigsy Ellingsworth right, Ken Germain mid. left, Dave Rebeor mid. right, Jack Henderson bottom left and Ray Smith bottom right.

These guys were the best of the best in the 50's and 60's.

David Rebeor was the best guitarist in Oswego, and he played with all the top local bands during that era. He was an exceptionally talented artist and teacher. David taught guitar at Gross Music Center and he played with one of my all-time favorite groups "Billy and the Barons" (pictured.) The band featured vocalist Billy Cook who was a very attractive young man and a great talent. He was taken from us far too young.

Gigsey Ellingsworth was the sax man and he was great, Jackie Henderson played the drums and he was the best in the city.

Wherever Billy and the Barons played, the place would be packed, and Rock and Roll was at its best. They always played the block dances in front of City Hall and the crowds would be huge as the teenagers danced in the street to the great rock and roll tunes of the day.

The Valiants

Left; Richard Hillman; Buz Vandergrift, Sax; Sam Domicola, Vocalist; Dan Craft, Drums; Jack Connolly, guitar; and Jimi Losurdo, Oakley Guitar

There was a new generation of young, talented guitar enthusiasts in the neighborhood, initiated by the huge popularity of Rock and Roll. Next door to our house lived my good-natured fiend Billy Musacchio. A block up Third Street, lived Jimmy Losurdo, who would in later years take a professional name, Jimi Oakley. These men, along with Jackie Connolly, all became very accomplished professional guitarists. They spent their entire lives playing the instrument they loved and entertaining the people of Oswego and beyond.

Jackie Connolly had a younger nephew, David Dunsmore, who lived just around the corner from us next to Sheldon's on Van Buren St. between West 2nd and W. 3rd Street. He later became a very accomplished drummer and entertainer.

In the late 50's, you could hear them playing and practicing in the early evenings on Jack Connolly's front porch. The sounds of their guitars and amplifiers filled the air of the neighborhood for several blocks. No one ever complained because they produced very good quality Rock & Roll music which sounded much the same of as the recorded tunes they were playing. The young girls of the Flats would get up and dance in the street to the music while others would clap to the music and sing along.

I remember Jimmy Losurdo's parents purchasing him a magnificent Les Paul Jr. guitar. I was in awe of that guitar, as I was also interested in the stringed instrument. I can remember thinking what a wonderful gift from his parents because I believe it cost over three hundred and fifty dollars. That was the equivalent of three or four weeks of a working man's wages in those days.

Jimmy's Dad, Jim Sr., who I remember as a very good looking and kind man, had a great personality, and his mother Mary was a beautiful woman and equally nice. Both parents had already witnessed the great potential their young son possessed early on with his rapid growth at the Gross Music Studios, where the very talented Dave Rebeor taught him the mastery of the six-stringed instrument. Jimmy would become an excellent musician and dedicate his life to his beloved guitar.

Jackie Connolly, to my knowledge, never took a guitar lesson. He played by ear. Both Jimmy and Jack would play with some of the great Oswego rock and roll bands of the

60's and thereafter.

There were many others of that era who became excellent professional guitarists. There were also from the west side: Sammy Domicola and Richard Hillman, both great talents.

The east side produced others, including the most talented of them all, Buddy Murray (who also died far before his time) and Jimmy Dillabaugh, who was also an excellent guitarist. Jimmy spent his entire life playing and performing – and still does.

Several times a month, they would all get together at Jackie Connolly's front porch on West 3rd St. with their guitars and amplifiers. They would jam for hours and always drew a crowd of on lookers applauding and dancing in the street to every Rock & Roll song. The boys became professional entertainers in what seemed like overnight, but they had practiced long and hard every day before they took on the spotlight.

The people of the neighborhood were always very supportive. That was the nature of the Flats and the people of Oswego, to live and let live. Besides, their music was very good!

42 THE FAMILY REUNIONS

The Knopp Family Reunion Photo 1950

Sisters: Helen, Mary, Eileen, my Mom Frances in the black hat, many cousins also not pictured here. Little Doc Colasurdo in the farmer pants in the front row. (Not pictured: the Knopp Brothers Ben, Bill & Mickey)

We had our annual family reunions at Fair Haven Beach, a New York State Park about fifteen miles west of Oswego. This event to me always marked the end of the summer each year when the entire family would show up for a day of family gathering in late August. There were fun games, food and a day at the beach. It was always sure to be a fun time before returning to school and another soon-to-arrive cold winter.

The food was endless, and it seemed every family brought a huge watermelon, which never went to waste. It was a sight to see the young boys and girls eating a foot long slice of watermelon as the juice ran down the sides of their faces and arms. Then came the joy of seeing who could spit the seeds the farthest. We played games, ate and went swimming all day, and we had the greatest times with our family!

By noon, my dad would lie on a blanket under a shade tree and catch a well-deserved nap. Dad worked six days a week eleven hours a day and we were happy to see him rest.

As the years passed, it would become a great frustration and huge disappointment when, without any explanation (or at least we children were never given one) the parents just decided to stop having the reunions. I never understood why because we had such great times at those family outings at Fair Haven Beach State Park.

It is my personal and firm belief that family traditions should be maintained and passed on from generation to generation. These gatherings are so valuable to the strengthening of family, especially today when families have moved to all parts of the country and there are relatives that you will never see, or in many cases, never meet. To me, this was a very sad injustice when there were no more reunions.

43 A MYSTERIOUS DISCOVERY

On top of Van Buren St. Hill, a block west of Castle School was a wooded area that covered the full city block. It was bordered on the south by Van Buren St., on the north by Bronson St., on the east by W. 8th St. and on the west by Ontario St. It was just kitty-corner from the Diamond Match Park and baseball sandlot field. The block was densely wooded with very old and very tall 100 year-old trees. This wooded area was the scene for our battleground for our war games we played like, "The Americans vs. the Germans."

The German force was always led by Billy Gunther. Billy was a few years older than me, and he was always armed with a large heavy wooden rifle. Billy Gunther was, in my opinion, the original Rambo, a fearless soldier who would climb high in a tree and wait for his foe to come unexpectedly under him. Then he would leap from his perch high above the ground with a blood curdling scream and pounce on his prey.

I was once one of his unexpected victims, and I have to admit I was not all that crazy about the experience. However, it was a war game, and war was never meant to be pleasant. Being overcome by Billy Gunther in a war game was no disgrace, for he was a daring and worthy soldier in our war games.

One day, we were "at war" and I was in the thick underbrush in the northwest corner of the woods. I was near the corner of Ontario Street and Bronson Street. As I moved around this densely wooded area, I discovered a cave in the side of a small hill that led to a much larger underground opening and a tunnel.

This was a major discovery and demanded immediate exploration. As I crawled into the small opening of this cave, I was able to stand up in the passageway, which was about five feet high. The tunnel passageway had been blocked off with a brick and cement wall. This was a major setback that did nothing to calm my nerves. I was all alone in a cave and had no idea what awaited me inside. But, I was very anxious to know!

This was presenting a great dilemma. Why was this cave blocked off by a brick and cement wall? Why would someone go through the great effort to block off this passageway here in the woods? Why didn't they just fill the cave in with dirt?

There were so many questions that the answers could carry undesirable answers and potentially very bad consequences during further exploration.

I decided I would have to think about it before sharing it with anyone who might be too eager to attempt to knock this barrier down to discover why it was there. I was so curious about the unknown fate that would be on the other side.

I would have to sleep on this. This was a new experience for me to be cautious. Suddenly, I felt somewhat responsible and this feeling for me was a first.

That night I could not sleep at all. I was confronted by a nagging question: why was this cave here? Was this a secret tunnel going to the bowels of Castle School just a block away? Had it been used as a place of torture 150 years before, or a place for transporting slaves en route to Canada during the Civil War?

Was there yet another fort we didn't know about that was once here in the area of this cave entrance? Did the tunnel go down underground and under the river a mile away to Fort Ontario two miles away – like in the stories we had heard so many times before about that great river tunnel? Was it a stash for pirates to hide their bounties? The possibilities were endless, and I desperately wanted to know the answers.

For most of the night the one question that would not leave my sleep deprived mind was if there were a thousand sword wielding skeletons on the other side of the wall that had been instructed by some evil curse hundreds of years before to attack and slay any intruders that would dare enter the long since sealed off cavern? Just what was it that so needed to be protected that it had to be blocked off with brick and cement?

The next morning after my sleepless night of tossing and turning, I decided this was an adventure that needed to be left alone, at least for the time being.

I would share the cave with the gang. However, I told them that someone had a very good reason for going through the great trouble of placing that brick and cement wall inside that cave. I, for one, had no desire to find out why. We never did try to knock that wall down to find out the answer to that mystery.

To this very day, this was one thing that has haunted me throughout my childhood. I never found out what the answers were to all these questions because we never knocked that dammed wall down.

It is a fact that some things in life are just better off left alone. In my mind, the cave in the forest on top of Van Buren Street hill with the unexplained and very strange brick wall was one of them.

44 THE HIGH SCHOOL YEARS

Oswego Public High School

High school in the "Glory Years" of the early 1960's was an exciting time filled with many memorable events and special moments. There were exciting sporting events, dances and the cultivated friendships that would last a lifetime. It was our indoctrination to new things. It was our coming of age. It was a time for making choices that could have profound effects on our lives and future.

Our main objective as we saw it in those days was to have fun. Everything else was a distant second. James Dean and Rock & Roll assured us our rebellion was good.

I, like many of my friends, would always put too much emphasis on the fun aspect of choice and not enough on the possible negative results of that choice. Of course that wasn't always the intelligent consideration because "Murphy's Law" was always in full force and bad decisions would always end with undesirable, bad and sometimes painful results.

There were the beach parties in the evenings with huge bonfires, beer and rock & roll music filling the air.

There were the first romantic interludes that sent our hearts to pounding with excitement and the confusion because we were somewhat scared because we didn't really know what to do.

Some of the romances would lead to a future marriage with high school sweethearts and a love affair that would last a lifetime. Others would be the first of many and labeled puppy love.

In 1963, after months of me haunting him, my cousin Ron Verdoliva sold me his beautiful, immaculate, blue two-tone 1957 Ford convertible. This was a beautiful car and it was in excellent condition, complete with a brand new convertible top. I was in awe of this car.

I had saved all the money I had ever made from all my jobs growing up. My father was the General Manager of the Oswego County Cleaners and he hired me for some cleaning jobs. My job duties were to wash the massive windows that surrounded the Fulton, NY pick up station and Laundromat, mop the floors and general cleaning at that location every weekend.

I did such a good job at the Fulton store that my dad's boss, Charles Bonsack, had my dad hire me to do the huge storefront windows at the main store on East Bridge Street in Oswego. I really never understood what was the big deal about washing windows. It certainly isn't a difficult task, nor does it really require any particular skills. However, Mr. Bonsack loved the looks of the windows when I finished. It made my dad proud that I did a good job, so that made me happy. Of course, the additional income was great to have, too.

Every Saturday and Sunday morning at 7:30 a.m. my father would drive me to the Fulton store. He would then pick me up at 5:00 p.m. I would religiously save every penny I earned. At the time, I didn't know what I would use the money for, but I was certain it would be for something very special.

My cousin Ron's convertible would be that choice. This beautiful car was an automobile that anyone would be very proud to own. For a seventeen-year-old high school student, it was an absolute dream car and I could not have been more proud to be its owner.

Cousin Ron was an excellent auto mechanic at Barilla's Rotary Station near the forks of the road, and he kept his beautiful car in excellent running condition as well as sparkling like a precious gem at all times.

The beautiful convertible was originally an automatic transmission but Cousin Ron replaced the automatic transmission with a manual transmission and a three speed Hurst floor shift, making it even cooler, and adding to its already great appeal – especially to a teenager living in a time of hot rods and floor shifts.

I was absolutely over the moon when he sold me this magnificent automobile. I could be seen cruising Bridge St., the main drag in town, with top down, sitting tall on the vinyl bench seat with my left arm resting on the highly polished two tone blue door.

I would cruise back and forth the main drag on Bridge Street so often that the old timers who sat along the side of Bridge Street perched on their benches would look up and say, "Here comes the nut in the blue convertible again, wasting more gas." These old boys would just shake their heads as I passed by again and again. They were of course rough old cobs from the old days who knew my car and me by name, although I had never been introduced to any of them. This is one questionable virtue of small town living.

At times when traffic was backed up, I would drive by the old boys ever so slowly. I would hear them and chuckle to myself thinking that I must provide a great deal of entertainment for the old boys as they would shake their heads and chuckle as I cruised by for the tenth time that day. I never failed to nod to acknowledge the old gentlemen.

I could not help but grin as I drove by them a dozen times a day and watch them chuckle at the kid in the blue Ford convertible with nothing better to do than cruise the main drag. After all it, was at a cost of twenty-five cents a gallon. And who could afford that, especially a high school kid?

When going from high school to football or baseball practice at Leighton Field, my car would be loaded with young athletes as we pulled into the Leighton School parking lot for practice or a game.

It was a given within our gang of jocks that once a week on Saturday afternoons after our varsity ball game had finished, we would drive around the corner to Barbara's IGA at the Forks of the Road and load the trunk of the convertible with beer, ice, hot dogs, buns and a large jar of mustard. We would then head for Sheldon's beach, which was not even a mile away. We would build a huge bonfire where we would cook our hot dogs and drink our beer as the car radios blasted out Rock & Roll.

We would feed the bonfire with tons of driftwood we would collect from along the beach that had washed ashore and dried out long ago.

As the flames and sparks lit up the night's black air and reflected off the lake water, we would dance uncontrollably like warriors preparing for battle. It was a wild time in paradise and it was the greatest time of our lives. We loved every minute.

I do have to admit that our group was a small contingency that was definitely considered to be somewhat of a wild group of outcast teenagers, but we didn't care. We were letting our emotions do what they would and we were carefree having the time of our lives.

There were several of our friends that participated that were not athletes, but they loved to party on the beach with the free spirits, and they never missed a Saturday bonfire.

45 THE CONVERTIBLE JOCKS

Leo Mc Sweeney was a good friend and very well-liked by everyone in school. He had an attractive – make that beautiful – sister Julie. They shared a very sharp blue 1962 Buick convertible their dad had purchased for them from Ebert Buick on East Bridge Street. It was a beautiful car.

Bobby Axtell (BA) had a 1956 orange-colored Oldsmobile convertible and all three convertibles could be seen cruising all over town looking for fun and adventure. We never failed to find it.

Bobby Axtell, or "BA," was one of my all-time favorite characters in high school because he could be counted on to create some excitement. He had a great sense of humor, as did we all. Bobby was better known as B.A., which he would be quick to point out stood for "Bad Ass." Between the three convertibles, we could carry all of our gang, which was some of the varsity athletes and several of our loyal friends.

46 OUR FAVORITE WATERING HOLES

We had three favorite watering holes in which the proprietors were very lax when it came to checking ID to see if you were eighteen, which was the legal drinking age at the time to consume alcohol. There was Ralph's Place on West Bridge St. just a few doors east of Woods Bar and Grill and just two hundred yards east of the Forks of the Road. That was one of our regular stops. However, our favorite bar was Jack's Place on the corner of West Liberty and West Schuyler Street. It was run by old Jack Phillips, who was one of my all-time favorite characters.

Old Jack Phillips was a rough old cob who was passionate about New York Yankee Baseball and would not hesitate to enforce his no noise rule during a Yankee broadcast upon any customer creating a disturbance during a Yankee broadcast.

MICHAEL J. COLASURDO

Jack's Place – 1940

Spagg Busky (L) and Jack Phillips (R)

In 1963, our gang would spend most of our time at Jack's Place. Jack was a salty old hardcore barman and his best friend and customer was old Spagg Busky, who was a fixture at the corner of the bar. He was, without question, the greatest character I have ever met.

Jack always had within his reach a twenty-inch long mahogany club that was a solid two inches in diameter just in case anyone became too rowdy during his beloved Yankee baseball games. Jack had an old and weathered small bar TV and an old radio that were both set on Yankee broadcast stations. Anyone making an attempt to change either channel would soon wish they hadn't, because that was far more than old Jack could tolerate.

I can recall young Bobby Axtell being the first recipient of Jack's displeasure. BA never had much use for rules or restrictions to begin with and always seemed to push the envelope at any given opportunity. He loved to get a rise out of anyone anytime, especially if he had consumed more than a few bottles of beer. This was a major part of BA's charm. We knew he could always be counted on to create some great entertainment...and he never failed us!

As I said, Old Jack Phillips was dead serious about disturbances during a Yankee broadcast. At one crucial point during a game, BA, who had consumed several beers and had a loud piercing voice, for some reason went off on someone. That was more than old Jack could bear.

BA got whacked sharply over the head with Jack's "nasty stick," as we referred to it after that. It was a wicked hard blow that resembled the sound of a pumpkin being struck. For a second, I thought BA was going down for the count, but BA shook it off and started to yell at old Jack. Jack cocked his arm for a second assault on BA who hadn't yet understood the gravity of Jack's total displeasure of the situation.

BA was in shock and disbelief that this rough old cob would dare to whack him solidly upside his head. However, after quickly avoiding Jack's second attempt, BA stifled just in time as a few of the guys pulled BA back out of Jack's range and potential for yet another assault on BA's head.

When peace was finally restored the rest thought how funny it was to watch. However, BA never saw the humor.

By that point, Jack gave BA the ultimatum to either shut up or get out and never come back. BA chose to calm down for fear of yet another assault from Jack's club. He certainly didn't want to be barred from our favorite watering hole at Jack's Place.

From that day on, if we were in Jack's Place when the Yankees were being broadcast, you could hear a pin drop. This was alright with us because we were all great fans of the Bronx Bombers, too.

A few days later, I said to Bruce McDonald, Jimmy White, Leo Mac and Mike "Cooley" Cloonan, "Hey, guys, the Yankees are on tonight at 7:00. Let's get BA and go over to Jack's Place. We will buy BA some beers and see what happens." And we would all laugh!

Our gang's other all-time favorite character at Jack's Place was a legend in that part of town by the name of Spagg Busky, who I had personally admired for some time. I had met Mr. Busky several years earlier in my paper route days. I would always save Jack's Place for my final delivery.

Old Jack would always buy me a Coke, which I greatly appreciated after riding my bike and toting my paper bag full of newspapers on a hot summer's day.

After just one conversation with Mr. Busky, I found myself in awe of this delightful old gentleman. At the end of my paper route, I would hurry to Jack's Place with even more enthusiasm to get to take my place next to the wonderful character at the end of the bar. I enjoyed sitting near the large window to listen to this charming old man who possessed such great character.

Spagg's amazing life's adventures and truly fascinating stories were captivating. Spagg had a brilliant mind. He would sit with his legs crossed on his favorite bar stool by the big picture window at the front of the old bar and paint pictures with his elegant words that Mark Twain would have envied.

Oh, how I loved listening to that wonderful old man and the visions he placed in my head with his great stories. I would find myself sitting in his presence for hours and take those wonderful journeys through his past that he would describe as eloquently as only his words could.

I could never get my fill of that old gentleman's wisdom and wondrous stories. If you had ever known this delightful and charming old gentleman, you were deeply touched by his character, and soft demeanor. He commonly wore baggy beige pants, and a brown belt that he had cut a hole in the middle of so it would be tight enough to hold up his trousers. The belt hung down along his side almost to his knee. He also sported a dark plaid wrinkled shirt, a dark brown vest, an old weathered hat with its brim torn in a three places, and his classic walking cane. But he was always represented well by his unforgettable charm, his elegant words and his wondrous tales of life.

Before our caravan of topless cars made our routine stops at Ralph's Place and Jack's Place, we would drive out of town to another favorite watering hole, "The Pines Motel Bar" on Route 104 East. It had a great little bar and the owner never asked to see an ID card. Actually, I don't ever remember ever being asked for ID at any bar in those days. I guess the tavern keepers thought the 18 years of age drinking law was more of a guideline than an actual law because I never once saw any bar person attempt to enforce it.

In those days, most bars had bowling machines and The Pines Motel Bar had one of the best machines. It had room for six players to play at one time, as they all did. We would drink beer and bowl for a dollar a game, high man takes all. We would bowl for a couple hours as each game took about 30 minutes to complete.

I had these bowling machines down, and I won the great majority of the games. Jimmy Tripp and Butch Ferguson were very good players as well, and it would usually be between the three of us to see who would take the money.

Before we made our first stop out at the Pines Motel Bar, we would always put a couple dollars in a pool. We usually had plenty to buy enough beer, for they only cost 25 cents a bottle. We would buy a case at a time for about $5.00 to get the most for our dough. We would finish the case by the end of the second bowling game because there was usually about eight or ten guys in our bar hopping gang.

On the occasion that someone didn't have enough money, Leo Mac always seemed to be happy to contribute more than his share. He always had an emergency stash of cash, and he was never slow to share his generosity with his friends.

Leo was a standup guy who was well liked and respected by all. Leo and his family lived in a mansion at the city limits just south of town on old Route 48.

Occasionally, when Leo's parents would go out-of-town for a weekend, the word spread like wild-fire and there would be outrageous parties at their beautiful home.

On one occasion, Leo's parents (who never came back early or unexpected) came back home a day early and very much unexpected, right in the middle of a rock and roll deafening beer blast. They saw teenagers passed out on their lawn as they entered their circular driveway. It wasn't pretty for Leo and Julie on this day, as teenagers were intoxicated and falling down in the McSweeney front yard, which wasn't acceptable for the prominent and well respected family.

Leo and Julie's parents were really great and understanding parents, and in just a few days all was forgiven and well again at the McSweeney mansion. All restrictions were removed from Leo and Julie and we were all back on the road doing what we did.

I used to feel sorry for Julie because she never really partied with our gang, but she would always be part of the deeds if Leo got caught because she loved her brother and stood up for him at all times. I was always pretty sure her parents knew this, but they were always respectful of her loyalty to her brother and never mentioned that they knew. Leo was a great guy but Julie was a class act and I for one was well aware of that fact.

You would rarely see any of our gang without a smile on our face, a twinkle in our eyes and never without loud rock and roll blasting from the convertibles. We, like all teenagers of the 1960's, just loved to have fun, and oh, how we did.

It was very common to see the three convertibles cruising bumper to bumper with several teenagers aboard. I would often think to myself what are these old timers sitting on the sides of Bridge Street really thinking as we passed by, as they turned larger sticks into toothpicks. They would just briefly look up to grin, shake their heads and return to their work at hand.

47 FAIR HAVEN AND SORORITY CAMP

At the end of the school year, there was the greatest weeklong party of all parties, called "Sorority Camp." These legendary parties took place at Fair Haven Beach about fifteen miles west of Oswego on Lake Ontario. The convertible jocks would be there and the big party went on nonstop for a week.

There were many cottages for rent in the summer at Fair Haven surrounding the bay, and those were the camps the sorority girls would rent for the entire week.

At the end of each day, I would sleep in the back seat of my car after a long day of games, swimming and partying. I would sleep with the convertible top in the up position to prevent being eaten alive by the large mosquitos that left a welt the size of a nickel after dining on your blood.

One morning I awoke, yawned and stretched as I moved to the driver's seat and started the engine. I pushed the button to lower the top into its boot cradle behind the back seat when I heard what sounded like muffled screams coming from my trunk. I immediately returned the top to the up position.

In the boot of my car behind the back seat, was a small cubby where the top would fit perfectly when in the down position. One night, young Bobby Cole, who was small in stature, had crawled over me and into that boot. He slept there all night, like a baby in a cradle. When the top started coming down on him, he went into a panic and attempted to scream. Unfortunately for young Bobby, because of his alcohol induced state as a result of the evening activities the night before, nothing came out of his mouth. This caused even greater anxiety because of his inability to create a recognizable sound.

Fortunately for young Bob, I hadn't yet turned my radio on and I heard his panicked muffled cries. I quickly raised the top back to its full and upright position. He came scrambling out of that boot like a scalded dog in pursuit of instant relief. I just laughed. I could not imagine anyone sleeping in the small confinement of that boot. I was enjoying some belly laughs at this sight of the young man's scramble for freedom. Then I gathered myself and asked young Bobby how he had slept. In his broken and still raspy voice he said, "It was great until the top came down on me!"

We just laughed and went for beer, ice and some hot dogs and buns at the grocery store in town. They must have sold several thousand cases of beer that week! We then drove over to one of the camps where our friends would meet each morning to start another day's activities of games, swimming and partying to the sounds of deafening Rock and Roll music.

48 TIME OUT

By the morning of the fourth day of this weeklong party at Sorority Camp, I decided to call a time out and drive back home.

Upon my arrival home, my mother looked at me, gasped, and said, "What happened to you? You look like you could use a good meal and some sleep."

After a hot shower, my mother had the kitchen table laid out with some of my favorite things to eat. I quickly consumed everything. Then I went up to my bed and fell fast asleep for twelve hours. The next morning, Mom had made some spaghetti with meatballs and an apple pie.

After my shower, I was preparing to leave and Mom handed me two large grocery bags full of food for my return to Fair Haven and Sorority Camp.

She then asked me if I needed any money. I looked at the short woman and asked, "Is this a trick question, Mom?" We both laughed. Then the dear woman handed me thirty dollars. She had a warm and wonderful way about her and a generosity that was unmatched.

There was no question or doubt that my mother knew the money would not be put in a savings account for a rainy day, as she handed me the twenty and ten dollar bills. I hugged and kissed her and again thanked her. As I left, she stood in the door as she watched me back out of the driveway.

After a quick trip through the automatic car wash on West 3rd and West Utica Street, I headed for the working man's friend gas station on West 8th and Bridge Street to fill the gas tank. I then made one last stop at Barbara's IGA store on Route 104 just past the Forks of the Road to load two cases of beer on ice into the trunk. I was again off to Fair Haven and Sorority Camp, now rested, fed, refinanced, refueled and ready, willing and able to carry on.

As I drove along Route 104 East, I could only grin at the last vision of my dear mother in the doorway of our house as she watched me pull out of our driveway. She would shake her head as she usually did at my never-ending bad choices which she could just never seem to understand. However, the beautiful woman rarely put restrictions on or ever demanded much of me.

It was my mother's belief that a young person needed to make their own choices and learn by their mistakes. This was a problem for a teenage boy whose priority was having fun. I would always go with the fun choice, and naturally that would be the one that usually brought with it unwanted consequences.

We all love our mothers. However, this woman was without question a saint, and I adored her.

I was somewhat rebellious, and I suppose she did not want to have any confrontations with me, so she would just shake her beautiful head and allow me to do what I wanted to do. However, I would never intentionally do anything to hurt my mother's feelings, as I had enormous respect for the woman who was so kind and generous – especially to me.

Many years later I asked ask my mother why she rarely, if ever, put any restrictions on me during my exceptionally wild teenage years. She said, "Michael, if you don't try to choose your children's roads, they will always find their way home. "

Beautiful, compassionate and intelligent. I certainly understood why my father married this amazing woman.

When I arrived back at Fair Haven, the gang was happy to see the clean and shiny blue Ford convertible pull back in. When I opened the trunk, they started singing my praises and cheering their new found benefactor and bearer of food and ice cold beer.

Many of these young men were in desperate need of food, and they consumed half the food just as soon as they got a fire started to cook the dogs and burgers. For two more days, we had a great time at Sorority Camp swimming, dancing, playing and partying our asses off.

MICHAEL J. COLASURDO

49 AN UNEXPECTED DETOUR TO DESTINY

In 1964 Coach David E. Powers, Oswego's legendary coach, would step down after decades of creating a remarkable history and a winning tradition for the Oswego Public High School Varsity Buccaneers.

This would be a very difficult baseball season for the OHS Varsity Baseball team. It was even more difficult for me without the coach I had such great respect and admiration for, the coach who was greatly responsible for me becoming the very best baseball player I could be. In my life, some things had been difficult, but sports had never been one of them – until now.

I unfortunately had a history with the newly-appointed coach. I was what he considered a "rebellious kid from the west side." He refused to play me, and that was more than I could bear. Regretfully and very painfully, I quit the team. That was the hardest thing I had ever done in my life.

I was a highly motivated and competitive athlete, and this

would be the end of my athletics at Oswego High School. I was devastated at the time because all I lived for my entire life was sports. I was an athlete, that's who I was. Now who would I become?

For the very first time in my life, I was scared and insecure. With athletics, I was confident and now I was lost in confusion of who I would become. For the first time in my life, I was frightened to consider the future.

I had faced many challenges growing up. The greatest was being Dyslexic. This learning disorder was not understood – or even recognized – by educators in the 60's. Children with Dyslexia were labeled, "slow." I would grow to hate that term with a passion. Because I was Dyslexic, I struggled as a student, so my future as a college professor was highly unlikely.

As my frustrations were mounting, I decided I desperately needed a drastic change and a new challenge. I needed something at which I could strive to excel, a new direction, and a new challenge.

I was a competitor and I desperately needed to compete. With very limited options at eighteen years of age, I decided the biggest challenge would be to join the United States Marine Corps.

When I sat down with my parents at our kitchen table to tell them I had quit school and joined the Marines, my mother was openly upset. However, my father said, "This is not the end of the world. This will make a man of you. You just attack your duties as a Marine the way you attacked sports and you will be just fine. Just follow orders, use common sense and good judgment when you have to. Above all, don't do anything to piss off your platoon Sergeant."

Within a few weeks, I found myself at Paris Island, South Carolina at the Marine Corps Boot Camp Depot, better known as Marine Corps Boot camp hell, as all recruits discovered from their day of arrival. It was such a radical change in life. Life as a teenager was now a thing of the past.

I would now focus and become the best Marine I could be.

Although Marine Corps Boot Camp was considered by many to be hell, I was somewhat happy again, for my life once again had meaning and purpose. I now had direction, a challenge and a goal. Everything in boot camp is competitive to see how much you can adapt, improve and compete at everyday physical training, where you ranked in the competitions and who was the best at everything and anything we did.

It was great for me because everything we did was a competition to see where you ranked amongst all the others in your platoon and company. I was eighteen years of age and in excellent physical condition, and I was more than ready to compete. In fact, I was ecstatic to compete. I had found the challenges I desperately needed, and I would give my all to everything I did.

I decided that I would from this day forward and forever more accept full responsibility for any and all of my actions. I believe that was my first step in the process of becoming a man and reaching maturity.

Suddenly, and just like that, my life was no longer the same. I would now put away my high school lust for fun and I would focus and become one of the best Marines in Platoon 288 and I Company.

I gave everything one hundred percent, and my best efforts and I would excel to the top of my Platoon and I Company in all aspects of my training.

I fought fierce battles and became champion at pugil stick fighting in Platoon 288. I ranked second overall in I Company, number two of 290 Marines in I Company. Pugil sticks are simulated hand-to-hand combat with rifles and bayonets.

I was among 5 out of 77 Marines chosen to represent my platoon at the field events competition. I qualified with the highest possible ranking with firearms, "Expert" with M-16 rifle and 45 Caliber pistol.

I ranked in the top three percent of fastest times for all of I Company at the Confidence Course physical training efficiency course ratings. I threw a hand grenade farther than anyone else in my platoon threw, and again ranked at the top two percent in I Company.

At graduation, I was personally congratulated by each and every one of my drill instructors for a job well done. Staff Sgt. Ford, my senior drill instructor, told me that only Dick Strock ranked higher than I in platoon evaluation, and that I had ranked in the top three percent of 290 Marines in I Company – and that I should be very proud of that accomplishment.

The roads we travel in life are not always from choice but sometimes out of necessity. I became a Marine and that was the right choice for me. The Marine Corps provided the challenges and competition I so desperately needed.

My father had told me to attack the Marine Corps the same way I attacked sports and all would be fine and that's exactly what I did. My father once again proved to be right.

After a lifetime of accepting full responsibility for all my life's actions, I harbor no animosity towards my former coach.

That sudden and unexpected detour so many years ago delivered me to my rightful destiny and the wonderful life I have lived and for that, I am eternally thankful to him. The roads we travel in life are sometimes more of a matter of necessity rather than personal choice. However, somehow, someway we always manage to be delivered to our rightful destiny.

Finding our true destiny can sometimes take us down roads we might never have imagined traveling and the twist, turns and miracles of the journey that we experience along the way are the memories of our lives.

50 OUR SIBLINGS

They were our first best friends. There were the trials and tribulations and the mixed emotions of our everyday relationships with our siblings that could make us cry and laugh, sometimes at the same time. However, no matter how angry we might have ever gotten at them at times, we would love them throughout our entire lifetime in spite of any of our foolish childish differences.

There were the unforgettable memories of the great fun we shared together. There was the joy we experienced playing together inside the house on a rainy day or going to the ballpark and playing baseball for hours on end when the sun was shining. And there were the many other thousands of things we did together.

There were the games we would play that provided the competition that would built our strength and character. We loved competition because it was challenging, and we just had fun.

If you needed a helping hand, when you turned around, your sibling(s) were there by your side, never hesitating or faltering in your time of need. In spite of all the arguing and fighting that siblings do, they loved you and you loved them.

You and your siblings would fight, but if anyone else ever showed aggression towards your brothers or sisters, you would unite as a family against all others when needed to protect each other.

It was all about family, and that is what happiness and life are all about. Parents, siblings, spouse, children, and grandchildren, how could you ever expect to find true happiness without them in your life?

When you stop to think about the wonderful times of your life, your siblings were probably there with you, especially if it was during the 50's and 60's.

51 IT WAS THE GREATEST OF TIMES

All of the wonderful and unforgettable experiences that filled us with joy and happiness would be stored in the far corners of our minds, so that we could draw from these during the difficult times in our lives.

When we experienced difficult times, we would just stop and think about them and they would help us get through any tough times.

It is my belief that the older we get, the more important it is for us to draw from those joyful past memories and experiences, to rekindle the passions we once had for life as children, and to keep the excitement and joy of being alive present in our everyday lives.

Yes, it was the best place and time growing up in the small towns in the 50's and 60's. We were blessed growing up during the greatest time in all of history to be young and we lived it.

It has been my great pleasure to share these memories of my youth growing up in Oswego, New York. The seasons of our lives have changed many times, and I am now in the twilight of my years. But our childhood memories will always remain, as long as we dig deep enough to bring them back to the surface so that we can continue to enjoy them for as long as time allows.

It is my greatest hope that these stories will spark some memories of your own and will help to rekindle the events of your own youth that may have been shrouded in the darkness of time. You will be amazed at the chain reaction that will take place, one memory will bring back another and another and those memories will trigger others.

We all knew that one day we would all get old…we just never imagined it could possibly happen this fast.

I am deeply thankful that that I grew up in the greatest time in history to be young in the 1950's and 60's and all those wonderful memories of the good old days…

When we had it made!

Baby Boomer Brothers and Cousins

Frank Colasurdo, Ron Verdoliva, Mike Colasurdo, Ken Verdoliva

Oswego, N.Y. Harbor Sunset

52 A BRIEF HISTORY OF HISTORIC OSWEGO, NY

The Great Iroquois Indian Nation for 10000 years called the Oswego River the OSH WE GEH - A pouring out place

On the far northern end of New York State, there is a majestic river that is fed by the Finger Lakes of New York State. This historic river completes its final journey into the Great Lake Ontario at Oswego, New York; the name of this historic river is the "Oswego River."

This river is the second largest river to connect with Lake Ontario, second only to the great Niagara River. It deposits vast amounts of fresh water into the Great Lake Ontario, and has been the background setting for great novels written by such great authors as James Fenimore Cooper's *The Last of the Mohicans* and *The Path Finder*.

Remarkably, this watershed has been flowing continuously since the end of the last Ice Age, some 12,000 years ago, when the great mile high glacier came slowly sliding down from Canada and carved out all the Great Lakes and Finger Lakes. All the rivers and tributaries would later be filled with the water of the great glacier as it melted under the warming temperatures of planet Earth and the rains that would fall forever more.

I can recall as a young boy in the 1950's sitting on the west bank of this wondrous river, thinking to myself; where does all this water come from and why doesn't it ever run out? If you have ever been fortunate enough to sit on the river's shore or walked across the beautiful bridges, you may have asked yourself this very same question.

For many thousands of years, from 8000 until 1653 AD, the river at Oswego was the exclusive domain of the Iroquois Indians and "The Land of the Six Nations." The tribes of the Six Nations were the Mohawk, Seneca, Onondaga, Oneida and Cayuga. The Tuscarora would replace the Huron Tribe after being terminated during the Great Indian Wars.

In 1653 the First White Men Arrived in Oswego, N.Y.

In the middle of August in 1653, down the northern flowing Oswego River came several canoes guided by Onondaga Indians as they escorted two white men, the French Jesuit Priest, Father Simone Le Moyne and his woodsman guide Jean Baptiste, to the mouth of the Oswego River. The two men were making a return journey to Montreal, Canada after spending two years with the Onondagas where they had been on a mission to convert them to Christianity.

The Onondagas were assisting the two men as they returned from their village thirty miles to the south in modern day Syracuse, New York.

One of the lead canoes carried the two white men that was piloted by two Onondaga Indians, with several other canoes of Onondaga Indians escorting them to provide safety and protection on their journey.

Along the river their canoes glided effortlessly in the steadily flowing current of the river. However, as they neared the mouth of the river that poured into the great lake, a powerful windstorm was blowing across Lake Ontario, driving huge fifteen to twenty foot waves violently crashing into the eastern shore at the mouth of the river.

The Onongagas in the first canoe made signs to the others that they could no longer forge any further against the storm with its powerful and dangerous waves. They turned their canoe toward the shore to the west bank of the river and the others followed. All were soon safely sheltered on the shore of the river's west bank.

For two days, the small group of Onondagas catered to the man in the black robe, fulfilling his every need. As they camped on the shore, they could watch the storm as it continued to send massive waves violently crashing into the eastern bank of the river and exploding in a spectacular silver spray that sent the glistening water high into the air.

On the third day, the storm subsided, and the powerful waves became a gentle rolling surface of very small waves. The group loaded their canoes and continued their journey to Montreal along the southeastern shores of Lake Ontario, out the St. Lawrence River, on to the great Canadian city of Montreal.

Father Simon Le Moyne and Jean Baptiste were the very first white men to ever step on the shore at the mouth of the Oswego River. This took place in August of 1653 as noted in Father Simon Le Moyne's diary of his travels, amazingly some 10,000 years after the first Native Americans had arrived at the mouth of the great river and the southeastern shores of Lake Ontario.

At times as a young boy, I would sit on the river's west bank. Lost in young boy fantasies, I would picture in my mind many white birch bark canoes with several Native Americans, each with their long black hair decorated with white and gray tipped turkey feathers. They wore soft deerskin loin clothes that the women had labored over for hours to gain the soft leather texture.

The young braves carried a quiver of arrows strapped across their sun-darkened backs as they paddled against the never-ending current of the mighty river. It cast glimmering reflections of a thousand fall colors over the sun-sparkled waters from the multitudes of the huge 200 year-old trees that lined its banks. It all blended in perfect harmony. It was a breathtaking vision of a wilderness paradise.

In time, the Native American canoes would become but small images on the water. They would dwell in the shadows of the great French war ships that would send hundreds of six and twelve pound cannonballs raining down on the English occupied Forts of Oswego, raining down upon the land and its inhabitants, and plundering them into submission.

The first assault came from the French fleet under General Montcalm in 1756 during the French and Indian War. There were violent attacks on the Oswego forts that took place during the War of 1812 and during the Civil War.

Battles for dominance over the highly prized river and town were fought viciously. These battles brought on the bloodshed of Indians, French, Dutch, English and the colonists alike, who had once covered the land, and would fade ever so quickly into the flowing waters of the great river.

Oswego, New York was the northernmost outpost in America. It controlled the Oswego River, which was historically sought after because of its vital port and location for the dominance of New York, Lake Ontario and Canada.

The Oswego River was important because it joined several other bodies of water that extended through New York State, and joined the Great Lakes to the Atlantic Ocean at New York City. It was a vital maritime passageway and supply route that was far easier to navigate than the densely wooded forests of New York State, which did not yet have roads.

Many people would perish attempting to gain control of this vital water passageway and the little town at its mouth that flowed into Lake Ontario.

Oswego in 1795 through the 1800's would become the home of some of the finest skilled ship artisans. They would build the great wooden vessels of the day that would navigate the Great Lakes. These great ships were powered by the wind in their sails and the steam from engines that were fueled by the coal, later delivered by rail to the Port City of Oswego from the coal mines of Pennsylvania. The port city of Oswego, by 1820, would be known as, "The city where the rails meet the sails." It would also be one of the fastest growing communities in the United States of America during this time period.

ABOUT THE AUTHOR

Michael J Colasurdo - Born March 7, 1946, and raised in Oswego, New York, where he grew up in small town USA during the great Baby Boomer years.

Throughout my life, I have (like most) had to overcome adversity. As a child, I struggled in school as a victim of Dyslexia during a period when it was not yet recognized. That sent me down roads that I would not have imagined, and would deliver me to my destiny.

This effort has been my first attempt at putting my experiences to keyboard and hopefully not the last. My adult life has had many interesting twists and turns that have led to many exciting adventures laced with mystery, intrigue and danger.

I would like to thank you for allowing me to share my wonderful childhood memories with you. Hopefully they may awaken some of your own memories that may have been shrouded in the darkness of time and will bring a smile to your face and a feeling of happiness.

Our memories are our own life's stories.

As Capt. Augustus MaCrea said to his life long partner, Capt. Woodrow F. Call on Capt. McCrea's death bed in the greatest western ever made, *Lonesome Dove*.

"It's been one hellava ride, ain't it !"

And life is just that!

MICHAEL J. COLASURDO